PRAYER *for the* NATION

It's in your hands

MARY ERVASTI

© 2014 JASPER MULTICHANNEL LLC, MINNEAPOLIS, MINNESOTA USA

ALL DOMESTIC AND INTERNATIONAL RIGHTS RESERVED, INCLUDING THE RIGHTS TO REPRODUCE THIS BOOK OR PORTIONS THEREOF IN ANY FORMAT, WHETHER ANALOG OR DIGITAL. FOR INFORMATION, CONTACT:

PRAYER FOR THE NATION
Attn: SUBSIDIARY RIGHTS DIVISION,
P. O. BOX 123
CHANHASSEN, MINNESOTA 55317   U.S.A.

THE J-CROWN-SHIELD DEVICE IS A TRADEMARK OF JASPER MULTICHANNEL LLC.

FOR INFORMATION ON SPECIAL DISCOUNTS FOR BULK PURCHASES, PLEASE CONTACT PFTN WHOLESALE PROCUREMENT AT
1 – 877 – 337 – 1776
OR EMAIL
WHOLESALE-BOOKS@PRAYERFORTHENATION.COM

FIRST DIGITAL PRINTING – FEBRUARY 2014

ISBN – 13:   978-1495277474
ISBN – 10:   149527747X

To Dick, my dear husband, best supporter, and partner for life.

Acknowledgements

This book couldn't have been written without the support and help of my dear husband and closest friend, Dick Ervasti. He has taught, encouraged and pushed me to know myself and to be all I can be, not to mention all his work with the layout and the cover design and graphics. Thank you, Honey, and thank God I have you by my side forever.

Our close friend and Operations Manager, Annie Gehrke, has cajoled me, corrected my constant revisions, helped me manage our business and generally lent a hand wherever it was needed as she always does. Thank you, Annie, for your assistance, and consistent support.

To my dear friend, Kelly Will, who has taught me much about prayer, and who is a constant inspiration to me. Thank you for developing a prayer life that has helped me to learn.

Thanks to our good friend, Bonnie McDermid, who spent hours on several revisions as she edited this book. What a gift this is to us, Bonnie. Thank you so much.

To our friend, Penny Antonson, who keeps our home clean so that our mission can go forward, I appreciate you. Thank you Penny, for your help, dependability, and watchful eye over what needs to be done.

Thanks to Teri Secrest, Jan Weger, Deb Barbeln, Charlie D'Assario, Peggy and Gary McKeown, Bonnie McDermid, Janet McBride, Lisa Kittel, Rachel Schneider and Barbara Brown, who have been an integral part of our prayer team for years. Only God knows the rewards due you.

A special thanks to Barbara Brown, who has hosted our Tuesday night PFTN meetings. Your child-like faith has been such a gift to me.

Most of all, I thank God for being with me always, answering all my questions (at least when I ask them) and being my constant companion. You, Lord, are the restorer of my soul, and the One who constantly inspires me to be better and stay in my place, doing what You show me to do – no more, no less, lest I get in Your way or fail to do my part. I would never want to be in this world without You!

Mary Ervasti

Table of Contents

Foreword 9
Preface 11
To My International Friends 21
How to Use this Book 22
Introduction 23
Day I - *Foundational prayers and agreement* 27
Day II - *Armor, who we are in Christ, yielding* 29
Day III - *Honor, mind of Christ, leadership requirements* 33
Day IV - *Commitment, revelation, no limits* 35
Day V - *Awakening, teaching God's ways* 39
Day VI - *Forgiveness, self-examination, humility* 41
Day VII - *Study, thanksgiving, trust, debt* 43
Day VIII - *Strength* 47
Day IX - *Mercy, vindication, corruption, joy* 49
Day X - *Mighty men and women, led by the Spirit* 51
Day XI - *No worries, Integrity guides me, Psalm 91 is for my protection* 53
Day XII - *Declaring things in advance as though they've occurred* 55
Day XIII - *Yielding, repentance, new life* 57
Day XIV - *Prepared path, taking responsibility* 61
Day XV - *What's right, strength, trust in God* 65
Day XVI - *Labor, rest, clarity, giving, God's faithfulness* 67
Day XVII - *Not to worry, integrity, confidence, housecleaning, Israel* 71
Day XVIII - *Cheating, approval, submission, life and death* 75
Day XIX - *Idols, rooted and grounded, wisdom, no condemnation* 79
Day XX - *Casting cares, undaunted, standing up, your voice* 81
Day XXI - *Same measure of faith, seek first the Kingdom* 85
Day XXII - *Grace and mercy, terrorists, negative passions* 89
Day XXIII - *Promises, false reports, bribes, canceling assignments* 91
Day XXIV - *The U. S. Constitution; Unshakeable, judges,
    laws established by the people* 95
Day XXV - *Hundred-fold return, liars destroyed, honor* 99
Day XXVI - *Love your neighbor, depart from sin, do God's commands* 101
Day XXVII - *Justice, blessing, established and steady, judges* .. 103
Day XXVIII - *Falsely accused and defended by God* 107
Day XXIX - *God will never leave us, repentance, protection* 111
Day XXX - *Reverence, hypocrisy, envy* 115
Day XXXI - *Arrogance, political correctness, continuous supply* 117

Appendix A, *The Declaration of Independence* 121
Appendix B, *THE UNITED STATES CONSTITUTION* 129
Appendix C, *The Constitution (additional notes)* 157
Recommended Reading/Listening/Viewing List 159
Lexicon of terms 163
Salvation Prayer 164

Foreword

In this era of time, when most all news reported is bad news and complaining is a way of life, Mary Ervasti hits the nail on the head, "Stop complaining and start praying!" That was my immediate reaction to this book.

We have been taught the power of speaking and declaring God's Word. As Jesus said, in Matthew 11:23-24, we have faith to move mountains. So why aren't we directing our faith-filled words to change this nation? Did we think "they" (someone else, somewhere) were taking care of "all that" for us?

For the nation to change, we must change. My father, Charles Capps, says that "faith comes by hearing yourself speaking what God said." In other words, we must take responsibility for speaking God's Word and saying what He said. No one is going to do it for us, we are the ones who determine what comes out of our mouth.

In this book, Mary sets forth the declarations from God's Word that will change us and will change the nation as those words of power are released in the realm of the spirit.

Let's stop calling it like it is, and call it like we want it to be!

Annette Capps
January 19, 2014

Prayer For The Nation - Mary Ervasti

Preface

Reasons for this book

I wrote this book because I believe it is time for all Americans to have a simple way to pray together for our nation. I also want to give us all one more way to harness the power of the prayer of agreement.

As we all pray these prayers, we can stand in agreement with each other in our hearts, and create a better world because of the promises of Jesus Christ. These prayers also come out of my own prayer for my nation, the prayers and intercession of those I have prayed with, and the motivation we have received from seeing answers to our prayers.

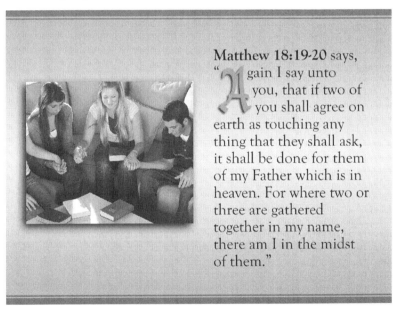

Matthew 18:19-20 says, "Again I say unto you, that if two of you shall agree on earth as touching any thing that they shall ask, it shall be done for them of my Father which is in heaven. For where two or three are gathered together in my name, there am I in the midst of them."

Since all power in heaven and on earth was given to Jesus and He made us joint heirs to that power, we in the body of Christ (anyone who has received Him as Savior and Lord) have access to all power in heaven and in earth through the name of Jesus Christ, and under His direction.[1]

---
1 *Matthew 28:18; Romans 8:17*

Prayer For The Nation - Mary Ervasti

It is this power given unto men that is spoken of in the Declaration of Independence.[2] Power comes from God and not from men. As you will see in the prayers that follow, God has much to say about how that power is used. He blesses those who use it wisely and punishes those who don't. All these promises from God are ours for the taking. However, as you will see, God does not act without us.

Our part is to hear from Him, speak what He says and do it with His power, believing He will do the heavy lifting for us. This is not hard. It only takes practice. Saying the prayers in this book (especially if you say them out loud, and especially if you stand and declare them as if you were taking the sword of the Word of God to our nation's problems) will build up your faith, your strength, and your resolve for the success of your nation.

Another reason for writing this book is that as I pray, and as I read the writings of our Founding Fathers, I know that the good and the prosperity that we have enjoyed in the United States for so long has been tied to a people who believed in God, obeyed Him, walked in His principles, prayed, listened for His wisdom, and did what He told them.

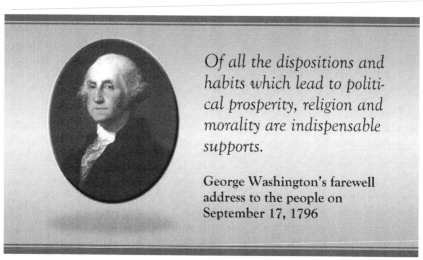

Of all the dispositions and habits which lead to political prosperity, religion and morality are indispensable supports.

George Washington's farewell address to the people on September 17, 1796

It's evident to me that people who follow that pattern are more confident, less afraid, more able to take risks, and more open to new ideas that improve a nation. It's my observation that those that do

---
2 See Appendix A

Preface

not walk in the confidence of God are of two camps. The first are afraid to take a risk, afraid they won't be able to take care of themselves, and are therefore prey to those who would take our freedoms in exchange for the promise of taking care of things for us. The second are the ones who prey on the innocent, prey on those who want something for nothing (or want others to take responsibility for them), those who are just going about their business and not seeing what's going on behind closed doors, and those who reject God altogether.

This book is comprised of prayers of Scripture. We know we are praying in the will of God when we pray the scriptures and declare God's will over our nation in His own words. This process is very powerful. To have many of us doing this in agreement, all at once, will change our nation and our world as only God can change it. We are simply agreeing in prayer to that which He has already declared. The reality of conducting our lives with civility, honor, and a giving, godly spirit in our nation is ours for the taking. It's all in God's Word.[3]

Further, to borrow a sport metaphor, praying God's Word allows us to pray on the offense as well as the defense. God will speak to you as you say these prayers, and I encourage you to speak out in prayer what He tells you. He will put you on the offense and show you things that are to come so that you can pray that they turn out the way God desires.[4]

Praying by Faith

Some of these prayers may not be true for you at this moment, but you will notice that I have written them in present tense. That's because when you say these prayers—declaring them to be true right now - you are calling things that are not (yet) as though they already were, just as God did[5] and as Jesus did.[6] We are calling them into our life NOW, by FAITH. We are made in God's image so that we follow His example in creating what we need in our world.[7] We call things

---

3 Psalm 103:5; John 1:1
4 John 16:13; Romans. 8:26; 2 Corinthians. 2:10-11
5 Genesis 1:3
6 John 11:43-44; Romans 4:17
7 Genesis 1:27

as though they were right now by faith, and by the power in His word.

As you say these prayers, some of them may not make sense to you, but since they are all based on God's Word, they will build your faith if you continue to say them especially if you say them out loud. And what does faith do? Faith comes by hearing, faith works by love, and love never fails![8] In addition, if some of these prayers look like they are impossible to fulfill and way above your head, then take heart.[9] They are supposed to be higher and more powerful than we can imagine because they come from God! And since our national problems are larger than any of us can possibly imagine solving as individuals, we need to understand that this is the very reason for us to believe in God who knows all, and to continue praying, and staying in agreement with each other's prayers and with God's Word about it. We will need much more unity, cooperation and faith between us than we have seen. We need much more thought about what's good for the benefit of everyone than just what's good for ourselves. As for me, I expect to see more people doing impossible things through the power of God because of praying together like we are doing with the prayers in this book. Do you want to be one of them? I do.

You are Not Alone

Many of your brothers and sisters across the world are praying. I searched and found over 860 pages of websites pertaining to "Prayer for the/our nation" on Google alone.

See the **Recommended Reading List** at the back of the book for *Billye Brim's Live Streaming* worldwide prayer.

---

8 *Romans 10:17 Galatians 5:6; 1 Corinthians 13:8; Psalm 103:20; Romans 5:2-5*
9 Jesus said unto him, if you can believe, all things are possible to him that believes. And straightway the father of the child cried out, and said with tears, Lord, I believe; help my unbelief. *Mark 9:23*

Preface

A government of the people

When you read and say these prayers, you may think to yourself, "What has this to do with the nation? Why is this telling me that I need to clean up my life?"

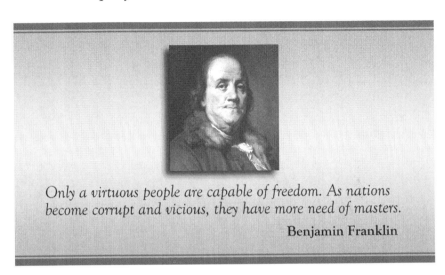

Only a virtuous people are capable of freedom. As nations become corrupt and vicious, they have more need of masters.
Benjamin Franklin

A nation is no better than its people. If we are going to have a godly nation, we must be a godly people. Further, self-governance requires a virtuous people in order to maintain freedom. We started out that way, but we are no longer a righteous people. Instead we have a faction that would take God out of our society, and that has led to our falling far from the heights we once had as a nation. As of 2008, the high school graduation rate of the United States ranks near the bottom among developed nations belonging to the Organisation for Economic Cooperation and Development (OECD). The OECD also reported that the U. S. was ranked near the bottom in science, math, and problem solving; and near the middle in reading literacy.[10] Even if some among us are virtuous, we have allowed our nation to fall from grace. God will judge the nations, and we will be responsible for ours.[11]

Malachi 3:5-11 says it this way:

5 And I will come near to you to judgment; and I will be a swift wit-

---
10 *Alliance for Excellent Education Fact Sheet,* March 2008
11 *I Corinthians 2:15*

Prayer For The Nation - Mary Ervasti

ness against the sorcerers, and against the adulterers, and against false swearers, and against those that oppress the hireling in his wages, the widow, and the fatherless, and that turn aside the stranger from his right, and fear not me, saith the Lord of hosts.

6 For I am the Lord, I change not; therefore ye sons of Jacob are not consumed.

7 Even from the days of your fathers ye are gone away from mine ordinances, and have not kept them. Return unto me, and I will return unto you, saith the LORD of hosts. But ye said, Wherein shall we return?

8 Will a man rob God? Yet ye have robbed me. But ye say, Wherein have we robbed thee? In tithes and offerings.

9 Ye are cursed with a curse: for ye have robbed me, even this whole nation.

10 Bring ye all the tithes into the storehouse, that there may be meat in mine house, and prove me now herewith, saith the Lord of hosts, if I will not open you the windows of heaven, and pour you out a blessing, that there shall not be room enough to receive it.

11 And I will rebuke the devourer for your sakes, and he shall not destroy the fruits of your ground; neither shall your vine cast her fruit before the time in the field, saith the Lord of hosts.

12 And all nations shall call you blessed: for ye shall be a delightsome land, saith the Lord of hosts.

13 Your words have been stout against me, saith the Lord. Yet ye say, What have we spoken so much against thee?

14 Ye have said, It is vain to serve God: and what profit is it that we have kept his ordinance, and that we have walked mournfully before the Lord of hosts?

15 And now we call the proud happy; yea, they that work wickedness are set up; yea, they that tempt God are even delivered.

I believe we are experiencing the judgment mentioned in verse five, and that we have gone away from God's ordinances in the Bible because we don't know what they are. We have allowed God to be spoken against, thrown Him out of our schools and out of the pub-

Preface

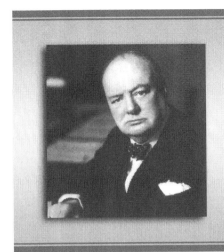

> We make a living by what we get; we make a life by what we give.
>
> Winston Churchill

lic square. Even so, God is still willing to work with us - but it's our move. When we return to Him, He will return to us.[12] Some would say we've been cursed as it says in verse 9. If so, we've allowed it to happen because we have left God; for there is no causeless curse.[13]

Furthermore, there is clear direction here as to how we can solve our problems:

- stop the sorcery, adultery, and lying
- stop oppressing the people in their wages
- stop oppressing widows, fatherless children, and strangers
- begin again to fear/reverence God
- return to God's way of doing things in the Bible — return to Him
- tithe on your income so that the church can take care of the poor and needy, so that the windows of heaven will be opened upon us, and so that we have more blessing than we could hold, so that God Himself would rebuke the devourer for our sakes, and so that we might again have abundance.

What happens in our nation is a collective response to what's happening in our individual lives.

Where government is concerned, we are a government of the peo-

---

12 *Jeremiah 24:6-8*
13 *Proverbs 26:2*

ple, by the people, and for the people. It is each one of the people's *intent* along with their *action* (or failure to take action) that makes things happen in our government. There are people who are in office for the benefit of the people, and there are some who appear to be there solely for the benefit of themselves. Each has their own intent, so we can't just lump the government together, and say, "They..." No, *we* are the government. It's our individual attitudes, faith, strength of will, and moral compass (or lack thereof) that are brought to bear as we elect the officials who are governing us. Therefore, I submit that our government is BY us, and whatever we uphold (or allow) as being right and acceptable is what we have. If we want something different, we have to BE different.[14]

We need to change

I have watched and listened to the news reports of the utter disrespect demonstrated across the political aisle in both directions. While many are angry about the handling of legislation such as debt, bailouts, healthcare, etc., we have no mandate to be uncivil and treat each other with disrespect. People acting dishonorably toward each other cannot possibly expect to get anything done. The polls show that the American people have little respect for Congress. That's true. However, let's look in the mirror. We elected them, and their behavior represents our own, or at the very least, our neglect of our responsibility to pray, vote, watch over, and guide the political process in line with our values!

Getting back to the basics

Church, we have been asleep at the wheel where our government is concerned. Since I was a child I have heard, "When are THEY going to do something about...?" Well, THEY didn't, and we didn't, so this is what we've got. You may throw up your hands and say they're all corrupt, but where will that get us? We all need to roll up our

---

[14] Do we know what our purpose is in life? Are we hearing from God about who we are, where we are to be, what we are to do, and what we are to say, so that we're in the right place at the right time doing the right thing for the right reasons? Are we developing the sovereign framework in God that will allow us to make the right decisions when it's up to us to make a difference? Have we developed the character to stand for what we believe even in the face of the strongest opposition, so that the perfect will of God can be done through us? It's time to ask God for help with these questions and get His answers.

Preface

sleeves, hear from the Lord about where to put our efforts, and do it. If we don't, then we can only look in the mirror to see who's to blame for what happens next.

Hear from the Lord

The good news is that if we are willing to persist in speaking for our values, willing to ask God what is to be done and how to do it, we will receive direction just as our forefathers did.[15] If you read about them, you'll understand why. They were men and women who studied the scriptures. God's Word has always been our greatest power, and always will be.

As we say these scriptures day after day, the power of that Word

Christianity is the companion of liberty in all its conflicts - the cradle of its infancy, and the divine source of its claims.

Alexis de Tocqueville

develops confidence inside us; a deep knowing that God really has thought of all of this before we were ever born. He knew the challenges we would face before the world was created, and He's made provision for these challenges. That's why He gave us His Word in the Bible. It's up to us to dig into the Word and stay with it until we get understanding.

Until then, we exercise our faith in God's wisdom, and trust He will direct us if we just keep listening, hearing, then knowing and doing as He says.

This I know. We can make the future of America better through praying together. Further, I believe our prayers in agreement, if consistent, will bring this nation to an even higher place than its former glory. *Prayer for the Nation* is not just for a short season; it is a lifestyle!

---

15 *Romans 8:14*

Prayer For The Nation - Mary Ervasti

I will pray for our nation for the rest of my life. I hope you will join me in this worthy undertaking.

Thank you for praying for the nation with me!

Mary Ervasti

To My International Friends,

Although I am American by birth, I believe prayer is universal. Furthermore, I see much of the world in the same kind of trouble that we've had here in the United States. Therefore, I extend to you the same agreement for these universal prayers to build up your nation[16]. We will all share the same heaven. We are all in the body of Christ as believers in the same God, and the same Savior, Jesus Christ, and the same Counselor, the Holy Spirit.

I bless you and your nation with the blessing to be fruitful and multiply in your prayers and your success! I look forward to meeting you in heaven if I don't get the chance to meet you here first.

Mary

---

16 *Matthew 18:19-20*

Prayer For The Nation - Mary Ervasti

How to Use this Book

This book is designed so that you can pray the prayers in sections. I have broken up the prayers into days - one for each day of the month. This way, you can say each of the prayers once a month. Those who choose to do this will be saying the same prayers with many others who choose to use these prayers for our nation by saying the prayers for each day of the month.

In addition, if you haven't yet made a practice of daily prayer, but have decided to buy this book because you know that the nation needs prayer, then this will help you establish that practice. It may also be helpful to set a time and place for prayer each day so that it is easy for you to establish the habit. With that being said, I would be blessed to be in agreement with you for however you decide to pray.

The book is also designed to build your faith with stronger prayers as you go further into the book. For certain prayers that seem outlandish or absolutely impossible, I have given you reasons why they can be accomplished, but don't just believe me. Believe God as you look up the scriptures that follow each prayer.

I encourage you to say these prayers out loud in an appropriate setting. Saying them out loud allows you to speak to your mind, your will, and your emotions as they hear you speak and take authority over your life. Your faith will increase with this consistent practice, and you will be able to see it in yourself.

You'll notice that some prayers are repeated or very similar but on different days. This is intentional because they bear repeating. There may be some that you decide to mark to be said every day, and I encourage you to follow whatever the Lord instructs you to do.

Most of all, you and I will be in agreement with many of our countrymen for the solving of the problems we face. No matter how monumental they may seem, you can make a difference. Together our prayers for our nation will help each one of us, and our nation as a whole. These words spoken out of our mouths will not return void, but will accomplish what God has planned for this nation[17].

---

17 *Isaiah 55:11*

Introduction
Our Biblical Basis for Success with these Prayers

A. Because all the prayers in this book are based on scripture, we are praying God's words, which carry God's authority; and, therefore, can expect God's results. We are in agreement with Him as Jesus was in agreement with the Father[18].

B. Scripture, or the Word of God, is a two-edged sword, which exposes truth and roots out evil[19].

C. The Lord's prayer is the template Jesus gave us to show us how to pray:

Our Father which art in heaven, Hallowed be thy name. Thy kingdom come, Thy will be done in earth, as it is in heaven. Give us this day our daily bread. And forgive us our debts, as we forgive our debtors. And lead us not into temptation, but deliver us from evil: For thine is the kingdom, and the power, and the glory, for ever. Amen.
Matthew 6:8-13

In this template we see:

- Recognition of God as Father
- Praise to God
- Agreement with God for His kingdom to come and His will to be done in earth as it is in heaven
- Asking forgiveness
- Recognition that we can't receive forgiveness unless we forgive
- Petition for help when we are tempted, and deliverance when only He can help us
- Recognition that it's His kingdom we are part of, He is sovereign (yielding to His authority), it's His power that we submit to and use under His direction, and we owe Him all the glory

---

18 *Matthew 18:19-20; John 12:49*
19 Let the high praises of God be in their mouth, and a two-edged sword in their hand. *Psalm 149:6*
For the word of God is quick, and powerful, and sharper than any two-edged sword, piercing even to the dividing asunder of soul and spirit, and of the joints and marrow, and is a discerner of the thoughts and intents of the heart. *Hebrews 4:12*

for it forever.

D. Because we take all of God's word as truth, and take Him as Savior and Lord over us, we then become a useful prayer warrior in the army of God, and can effect real change[20]. Our prayers then become answered because:

- They are based on the Word of God that contains the power to do what it says.
  John 1:1
- I apply faith to them and because God is in me.
  John 17:23
- My faith comes by hearing that Word repeated in my ears.
  Romans 10:17
- I am yielding to the love of God within me.
  2 Chronicles 30:8; Romans 6:19
- God does the work; I don't do this in my own strength because He is working in me to will and to do (work) of His good pleasure.
  Philippians 2:13
- I give voice to God's Word.
  Psalm 103:20
- God performs His Word.
  Jeremiah 1:12
- God's Word is His promise to us who believe, and He is faithful to His Word.
  Deuteronomy 7:9; Revelation 19:11
- I'm keeping God's commandments, and abiding in His love and love never fails.
  Exodus 15:26; 20:6; John 15:4-5; 1 Corinthians 13:8
- God has given us everything good.
  I Timothy 6:17
- I am an heir of God.
  Romans 8:17
- Life and death are in the power of the tongue.
  Deuteronomy 30: 14-15,19; Proverbs 18:21

---

[20] ... man doth not live by bread only, but by every word that proceedeth out of the mouth of the LORD doth man live. *Deuteronomy 8:3; Matthew 4:4*

- I yield to God and His ways.
  Psalm 40:8; Matthew 6:10

Prayer For The Nation - Mary Ervasti

Your Notes:

Prayers For The Nation
Day I
Foundational Prayers and Agreement [21]

1. Every prayer we pray from this book, we pray in the name of Jesus Christ of Nazareth, our Savior and Lord. We draw the bloodline around this nation, and declare the blood of Jesus protects her.
1 John 1:7; Matthew 18:19-20

2. Father God, I ask forgiveness for my past neglect to pray for this nation, for my pride and selfishness against my countryman, and for any sin I have committed that may have had an effect on the problems in my nation. I ask forgiveness for the unconfessed sins of my fellow Americans because we are to confess our faults one to another, and pray one for another, so we may be healed. The effectual fervent prayer of a righteous man (men/women/children/nation) avails much.
James 5:16; 1 John 2:1; 5:16; Romans 3:22

3. First of all, I pray for and give thanks for all people, all leaders, and for all who are in authority, that we may lead quiet and peaceable lives in all godliness and honesty.[22]
1 Timothy 2:1-2

4. I declare we are a blessed nation under God because we, the redeemed of the Lord, are the seed of Abraham, and all the nations of the earth are blessed who claim to be his seed. We are the redeemed and we say so.
Psalm 107:2; Genesis 18:18; Galations 3:9

---

21 Foundational prayers are appropriate to say each day if you choose to.
22 Timothy is making the point that before we pray for ourselves, our family or anyone, we need to pray FIRST OF ALL for those in authority over us because they have the power to influence our every day lives in the way we do business, whether we can pray in our schools or in the public square, and what we buy unless we take our authority in the Spirit to pray that they do the right and godly thing. Essentially, they have the power to enforce our freedoms or take them from us.

Prayer For The Nation - Mary Ervasti

5. We commit our government into Your hands, Lord, and we declare that we are one nation under God. Our government is free of officials that walk after the flesh in the lust of uncleanness, (are presumptuous, self-willed, not afraid to speak of evil dignities) and despise government.
2 Peter 2:10

6. I declare that the White House, the U.S. House, the U.S. Senate, and all courthouses and government buildings in the land are *our houses*. They belong to us as citizens and taxpayers of the United States of America. As for us and our houses, we serve the Lord.
Joshua 24:15

7. We stand in agreement with every person who is praying and believing according to God's perfect will. We lend our faith to their faith and receive their faith and agreement for our prayers as well.
Psalm 143:10; Isaiah 41:10; Amos 3:3; Matthew 18:19-20

8. You have heard our prayers, Lord, and we continue to gain victories one at a time. Help us to continue to remember that You are worthy of our trust. You are always faithful. The more we declare Your faithfulness, and the more we speak Your word back to You, the more the angels hear it and do the heavy lifting for us. It's our job to say it after You to get the ball rolling and to maintain momentum for our prayers. If we don't speak it in the earth, our blessings will remain in our accounts in heaven. We call those blessings to us now, and our collective voice is mighty before You!
Psalm 37:1-15; Matthew 28:18; Hebrews 1:3; Romans 8:17; Psalm 107:2;
Psalm 103:20; Isaiah 55:11

Your Notes:

Day II
Armor, who we are in Christ, yielding

9. Thank You, Jesus that You rule the world with truth and grace. That You make the nations prove "the glories of Your righteousness." We trust in You and do good, so we dwell in the land and have food. We delight ourselves in You, and You give us the desires of our hearts. We commit our ways to You and trust in You, and You bring forth our righteousness as the light, and our judgment as the noon-day. Thank You that we have major control and authority over this. There is a cause and effect relationship with You. If we do our part, You do Yours, Lord. Surely this is the "wonders of Your love!"
Genesis 1:26; Psalm 37:3-6; John 10:10;

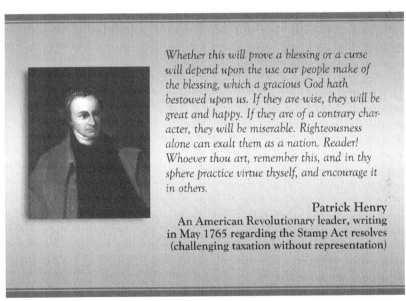

Whether this will prove a blessing or a curse will depend upon the use our people make of the blessing, which a gracious God hath bestowed upon us. If they are wise, they will be great and happy. If they are of a contrary character, they will be miserable. Righteousness alone can exalt them as a nation. Reader! Whoever thou art, remember this, and in thy sphere practice virtue thyself, and encourage it in others.

Patrick Henry
An American Revolutionary leader, writing in May 1765 regarding the Stamp Act resolves (challenging taxation without representation)

10. Everywhere I go today, God goes with me. Every thought I have today, God hears in me. Every problem I face, God is facing it, too. Every evil spirit I face, God is facing it, too, and He has already overcome it. He is in me and I am in Him. We are one spirit. I am the temple of the Holy Spirit.
John 17:21; 1 Corinthians 6:17, 19;

11. My tongue will proclaim your righteousness, Your praises all

Prayer For The Nation - Mary Ervasti

day long, Lord.
Psalm 35:28; Psalm 107:2

12. We put on the whole armor of God that we may be able to stand in the evil day and having done all, to stand. We stand with the belt of truth around our waist, taking the shield of faith so that we quench the fiery darts of the wicked. We take the helmet of salvation and the sword of the Holy Spirit – which is the Word of God. We play offense because Jesus has already paid the price for our success and has already defeated Satan, who is the root of all evil.[23]
Ephesians 6:13-17

13. Father, thank You that You know that I am dust. Thank You, Lord, for being so good, for Your mercy endures forever. Have mercy upon me, oh Lord. I will sing of Your power, I will sing aloud of Your mercy in the morning. You are my defense and refuge in the day of my trouble. You have shown me what is good, and what You require of me - to do justly, and to love mercy, and to walk humbly with my God. I commit to this, Lord.
Psalm 31:9; 59:16; 103:14; 1 Chronicles 16:34; Micah 6:8

14. I receive correction from the wise because it is better to hear the rebuke of the wise than for a man to hear the song of fools. I refuse to be quick to anger because anger rests in the bosom of fools.
Ecclesiastes 7:5, 9

15. I praise the Lord that I am blessed because I revere the Lord, and delight greatly in His commandments. I refuse to be afraid of evil tidings; my heart is fixed, trusting in the Lord.
Psalm 112:1,7

16. Lord, I choose to look back on my mistakes, and to recognize the times I went ahead on my own, thinking that I knew better than You. I declare that this self-examination motivates me to seek You first, and Your way of doing things, so that You may add things to me again. Above all, Father, add to me the ability and desire to yield to

---

[23] I literally stand and wield my sword (the Bible) and throw up my shield of faith as I say this prayer. You can do it too. You only feel silly doing it the first couple of times, but once you get into it, you will mean it with all your heart!

Day Two

You.[23]
2 Chronicles 30:8; Matthew 6:33; Romans 8:14

17. All the ends of the world shall remember and turn unto the Lord, and all the families of the nations shall worship before You, Lord.
Psalm 22:27

18. Thank You, Lord that we are free of the vexation and rage that kill the foolish man; jealousy and indignation slay the simple. Keep us free of the jealousy of the foolish, and the doom that follows it.
Job 5:2-3

19. I refuse to worry or fret about anything, but in everything by prayer and supplication with thanksgiving let my requests be made known unto God.
Philippians 4:6

20. You, Father, prepare a table for us in the presence of our enemies. Surely goodness and mercy follow us all the days of our lives and we dwell in the house of the Lord forever.
Psalm 23:5-6

Your Notes:

---

23 Puritanism would make every man an expert psychologist, to detect all makeshift "rationalizations," to shatter without pity the sweet dreams of self-enhancement in which the ego takes refuge from reality. A large quantity of Puritan sermons were devoted to…exposing not merely the conscious duplicity of evil men, but the abysmal tricks which the subconscious can play upon the best of men. The duty of the Puritan in this world was to know himself — without sparing himself one bit, without flattering himself in the slightest, without concealing from himself a single unpleasant fact about himself. Perry Miller, Puritan Historian *The Light and the Glory* p. 172

Prayer For The Nation - Mary Ervasti

Your Notes:

Day III
Honor, mind of Christ, leadership requirements

21. We honor God and His ways so that He honors us. If we reject and neglect the knowledge of His ways, we could be destroyed because people are destroyed for the lack of knowledge to do what's right.
1 Samuel 2:30; Hosea 4:6

22. Thank You God, for the birth of Your Son! Help us to remember that He came that we might have life more abundantly. This is Your Word, Lord, and I believe it and declare it to be so for me![25]
II Chronicles 20:20; Job 22:28; John 10:10; Romans 5:9; Hebrews 11:16;

23. Give us the mind of Christ, and help us to dwell on whatsoever things are true, honest, just, pure, lovely, and of good report; if there be any virtue, and if there be any praise, we think on these things, so that we rest in the power of God.
1 Corinthians 2:16; Philippians 4:7-8; Hebrews 1:3

24. I declare all leaders in this nation meet the requirements of God, so that all the people can lead quiet and peaceable lives in all godliness and honesty. I declare our leaders are able and God-fearing, that they are just, ruling in the fear and reverence of God, and above all, are truthful. Our leaders hate unjust gain, they refuse bribes, and are wise and understanding. They study to show themselves approved and able to know the truth. They are known for their good record of justifying things that are right and for condemning wickedness. Our leaders love justice and show no partiality in judgment, giving equal respect to rich and poor, unafraid of anyone's opinion except God's opinion of them. They are fearless, conscientious, strong, courageous, and obedient to the law.[26]
Exodus 18:21-22; 23:8; 2 Samuel 23:3; Deuteronomy 16:18-19; 1:13, 16-17, 25:1, 27:19;

---

[25] I believe the red of Christmas symbolizes His blood and the white His purity. His blood is what cleanses us and makes us white as snow. It is what saves us from His wrath.

[26] How can we pray like this? Because this is God's Word, not ours. We are giving voice to God's Word to bring it from heaven to earth on the wings of angels. It is our job to say it/proclaim it in earth as it is in heaven. In so doing, we bring heaven's blessing to earth as Jesus did. God will surely do His part if we do our part.
Psalm 103:20; Mark 9:23-24; Romans 4:17;

Prayer For The Nation - Mary Ervasti

Ezra 7:25; 2 Timothy 2:1-2; 2:15; Zechariah 7:9-10; Isaiah 5:22-23; Joshua 1:7-8

25. We follow Your ways, for affliction doesn't come from the dust, neither does trouble come out of the ground nor the curse come without cause.
Job 5:6; Proverbs 26:2

26. I refuse to let my heart be troubled or afraid. I walk in good cheer because Christ has overcome the world. I refuse to compromise because of fear. If I do, it means I don't believe the love God has for me, and what He is to me. If I cannot yet believe this, then I choose to strengthen my faith by declaring that I have the faith to believe.
Genesis 15:1; Psalm 34:4; Job 22:28; John 14:1; 16:33; Romans 10:17, 4:17

27. I seek God, inquire of God, and commit my cause to Him Who does great and unsearchable things, marvelous things without number, Who gives rain upon the earth and sends waters upon the fields, so that He sets on high those who are lowly, and those who mourn He lifts to safety.
Job 5:8-11

28. We take heed to these statutes and ordinances [in the Bible]. We guard our lives diligently, lest we forget the things which our eyes have seen and they depart from our [minds and] hearts, but we teach them to our children and our grandchildren.
Deuteronomy 4:9

Your Notes:

Day IV
Commitment, revelation, no limits

29. The scriptures have taught us statutes and ordinances as the Lord our God commands, and we declare we do them in the land which we possess. We keep them and do them, for that is our wisdom and our understanding in the sight of the peoples who, when they hear all these statutes, say, "Surely this great nation is a wise and understanding people."
Deuteronomy 4:1-9

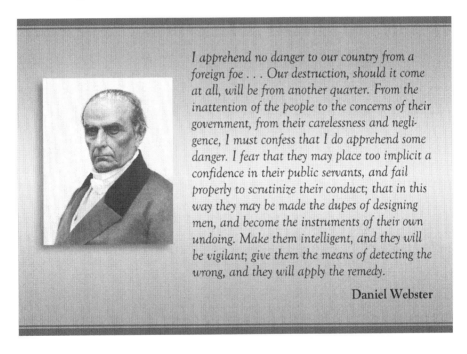

I apprehend no danger to our country from a foreign foe . . . Our destruction, should it come at all, will be from another quarter. From the inattention of the people to the concerns of their government, from their carelessness and negligence, I must confess that I do apprehend some danger. I fear that they may place too implicit a confidence in their public servants, and fail properly to scrutinize their conduct; that in this way they may be made the dupes of designing men, and become the instruments of their own undoing. Make them intelligent, and they will be vigilant; give them the means of detecting the wrong, and they will apply the remedy.

Daniel Webster

30. We pray one for another that we may also be healed.
James 5:16

31. We rejoice and exalt in hope, are steadfast and patient in suffering and tribulation, and are constant in prayer.
Romans 12:12

Prayer For The Nation - Mary Ervasti

32. Thank You, Lord that You have made known to me what I desired of You because You reveal the deep and secret things and You know what is in the darkness.
Daniel 2:20-23

33. Every person who calls evil good and good evil is heading toward destruction. Those that are upright rise as light in the darkness, are gracious and full of compassion, doing what is right before God. For nothing is secret that will not be revealed, nor anything hidden that will not be known and come to light.
Psalm 112:4; Isaiah 5:20; Luke 8:17

34. God frustrates the devices of the crafty, so that their hands cannot perform their enterprise or anything of [lasting] worth. He catches the [so-called] wise in their own trickiness, and the counsel of the schemers is brought to a quick end.
Job 5:12-13

35. I am happy and fortunate when God reproves me, and I do not despise or reject the correction of the Almighty even if it temporarily subjects me to trial and suffering. For He wounds, but He binds up; He smites, but His hands heal. He rescues me in six troubles; in seven, nothing that is evil will touch me. In famine He will redeem me from death, and in war from the power of the sword. I am hidden from the scourge of the tongue; neither shall I be afraid of destruction when it comes.
Psalm 112; Job 5:17-22

36. I am not limited by man's limitations, but I make my tents large. I spread out! I think big! I drive the tent pegs deep. I'm part of bringing my nation back to its foundations. I refuse to be afraid or embarrassed. I refuse to hold back and refuse to allow political correctness to muzzle me, so that my descendents and I possess this nation.[27]

---

[27] Dr. Jedediah Morse (1761-1826), was a pioneering American educator and geographer called the "Father of American Geography." He was also the father of Samuel F. B. Morse, inventor of the telegraph and "Morse Code." In 1784, after having taught in New Haven schools for several years, Jedediah Morse was dissatisfied with the deficient, inaccurate geographic information about America contained in the only available textbooks, which were European. Therefore Morse compiled and published the first American geography book under the title of

Day Four

Isaiah 54:2-3; Deuteronomy 26:18-19; 2 Corinthians 4:13

To the kindly influence of Christianity we owe that degree of civil freedom, and political and social happiness which mankind now enjoys. In proportion as the genuine effects of Christianity are diminished in any nation, either through unbelief or the corruption of its doctrine, or the neglect of its institutions; in the same proportion will the people of that nation recede from the blessings of genuine freedom, and approximate the miseries of complete despotism... All efforts made to destroy the foundations of our holy religion ultimately tend to the subversion also of our political freedom and happiness. Whenever the pillars of Christianity shall be overthrown, our present republican forms of government, and all the blessings which flow from them, must fall with them ...

Jedediah Morse

Your Notes:

Geography Made Easy. Read more at:
http://pftn.co/bJies
-and-
http://pftn.co/10RoK
 Now thanks be unto God, which always causes us to triumph in Christ, and makes manifest the savor of His knowledge by us in every place.
2 Corinthians 2:14

Prayer For The Nation - Mary Ervasti

Your Notes:

Day V
Awakening, teaching God's ways

37. Prove the glories of Your righteousness[28] in us again, Lord, making our nation a world leader because we choose to be a righteous[29] people before You.
Jeremiah 4:2

38. We are building You an altar Lord, declaring Your righteous Word as our own, knowing that You are working through us.
Colossians 1:27

39. We BELIEVE the Hero born of woman, Christ Jesus, has crushed the serpent's head with His heel, that He is sifting out the hearts of men before His judgment seat, and our souls are swift to answer Him, our feet jubilant to obey, knowing that our God marches on in us. We are the body of Christ, the soldiers of the army of God.
Genesis 3:14-15; Exodus 23:22; Colossians 1:24

40. We choose to understand and allow the glory of God to truly transfigure us so that, because He died to make men holy, we can live to make men free, praying His Wisdom into the mighty, and His relief to the brave. Thank You for working through us, Father. Let us be clean vessels for You to work through. Glory, glory, hallelujah![30]
1 Corinthians 15:3; Ephesians 1:18; 2 Peter 1:3; Jeremiah 9:23-24; Colossians 1:27

41. I declare that our nation has an awakening to God so that we can be the light to the world that God has called us to be.
Job 22:28; Joel 3:12; Matthew 5:14; Romans 13:11-14

42. Help us to teach Your ways to others as You prompt us, and prepare their hearts to receive it according to Your perfect will, because to love wisdom is to bring good to ourselves.

---

28 In the Christmas carol, "Joy to the World," I was struck by the words "And makes the nations prove the glories of His righteousness." (You can find the lyrics at: http://pftn.co/YAiyH)
29 Doing things at the right time, the right way, for the right reasons because they're right.
30 We're confessing/declaring by faith because we have asked the Holy Spirit to come into us. He does the work as we yield to Him within us. *Romans 4:17*

Prayer For The Nation - Mary Ervasti

Genesis 18:19; Ezra 7:25; Proverbs 4:5-7; 16:16; 19:8; James 1:5

The Battle Hymn of the Republic

Mine eyes have seen the glory of the coming of the Lord:
He is trampling out the vintage where the grapes of wrath are stored;
He hath loosed the fateful lightning of His terrible swift sword:
His truth is marching on.

(Chorus)
Glory, glory, hallelujah!
Glory, glory, hallelujah!
Glory, glory, hallelujah!
His truth is marching on.

I have seen Him in the watch-fires of a hundred circling camps,
They have builded Him an altar in the evening dews and damps;
I can read His righteous sentence by the dim and flaring lamps:
His day is marching on.

I have read a fiery gospel writ in burnished rows of steel:
"As ye deal with my contemners, so with you my grace shall deal;
Let the Hero, born of woman, crush the serpent with his heel,
Since God is marching on."

He has sounded forth the trumpet that shall never call retreat;
He is sifting out the hearts of men before His judgment-seat:
Oh, be swift, my soul, to answer Him, be jubilant, my feet!
Our God is marching on.

In the beauty of the lilies Christ was born across the sea,
With a glory in His bosom that transfigures you and me:
As He died to make men holy, let us die to make men free,
While God is marching on.

He is coming like the glory of the morning on the wave,
He is wisdom to the mighty, He is honor to the brave;
So the world shall be His footstool, and the soul of wrong His slave,
Our God is marching on.

Julia Ward Howe
Written in November 1861 and first published in
The Atlantic Monthly in February 1862.

Day VI
Forgiveness, self-examination, humility

43. Father, forgive us our sins, and the sins of our nation. You have said we may come boldly to the throne of grace, and obtain mercy and grace in time of need. We ask for Your help, Lord, and we believe in You. We trust in You, we know You hear our prayers, and that You answer them.
Hebrews 4:16; 1 John 5:16;

44. We refuse to be deceived, deluded, or misled; God will not allow Himself to be sneered at (scorned, disdained, or mocked by mere pretensions or professions, or by His precepts being set aside.) We inevitably delude ourselves if we attempt to delude God. For whatever a man sows, that is what he will reap. Therefore, we refuse to sow to our own flesh (lower nature, sensuality — what our senses want). which leads to decay, ruin, and destruction, but we sow to the Spirit and from the Spirit we reap eternal life.
Galatians 6:7-8

45. I focus on the things that are true, honest, just, pure, lovely, of good report; if there be any virtue, or any praise, I think on these things. I refuse to talk about all the negative things, but I enjoy my life because You have given us all things to enjoy.
1 Timothy 6:17-25

46. Father, we dedicate ourselves to consistent (if not daily) self-examination. We cast out every thought or imagination that exalts itself against our knowledge of You, because we understand that every thought and action sown is what we will reap. Help us to sow seeds of repentance, forgiveness, humility, love, kindness, joy, laughter, and giving, so that the atmosphere in our nation would be filled with the positive vibration of these thoughts and actions, and that we would never have to fear reaping what we have sown.
2 Corinthians 10:5

47. We refuse to be unwise, but listen to and understand what is the will of the Lord.
Ephesians 5:17; Romans 8:14

48. Father, you said if we would humble ourselves, pray, seek Your face, and turn from our wicked ways, then You would hear from heaven, forgive our sin, and heal our land. We, the redeemed of the Lord, commit to doing all of these things and declare that You are redeeming us from the hand of the enemy.
2 Chronicles 7:14; Psalm 107:2

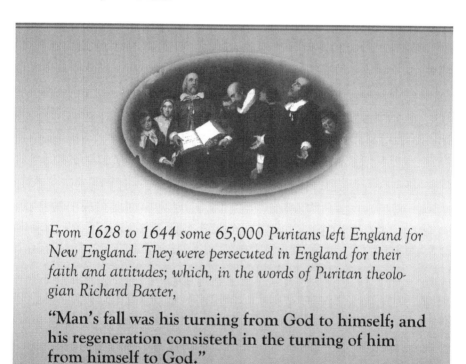

From 1628 to 1644 some 65,000 Puritans left England for New England. They were persecuted in England for their faith and attitudes; which, in the words of Puritan theologian Richard Baxter,

"Man's fall was his turning from God to himself; and his regeneration consisteth in the turning of him from himself to God."

Day VII
Study, thanksgiving, trust, debt

49. I study to show myself approved unto God. I am the person who makes my voice heard by speaking what the Lord has given me and I speak the Word in His timing. I am not ashamed of the gospel of Christ for it is the power of God to save us.
Isaiah 50:2-10; Mark 13:11; 2 Corinthians 4:13; 2 Timothy 2:15; Revelation 1:16; 8:14; 12:11

50. From now on, we thank You, Lord, for Your answers to our prayers, and stand believing and expecting to see You move. We know you heard us the first time we prayed. Now we thank You for all You're doing that we cannot see, and for all You have already done and what You will do. You are the Way!
John 14:6; Philippians 4:6

"...*let us humbly commit* our righteous cause to the great Lord of the Universe, who loveth righteousness and hateth iniquity. And having secured the approbation of our hearts by a faithful and unwearied discharge of our duty to our country, let us joyfully leave our concerns in the hands of Him who raiseth up and pulleth down the empires and kingdoms of the world as He pleases..."

*John Hancock's prayer on March 5, 1774 to commemorate the Boston Massacre.
Deuteronomy 8:20; Isaiah 23:11; 37:16; Zephaniah 3:8; Daniel 2:21

* *Original Intent*, Wallbuilder Press, 2000, pp 91

51. We pour out our hearts before You, Lord, trusting, leaning on, and relying on You in confidence, knowing that You are our Rock and our Salvation. You are our Defense and our Fortress. We will not fall from our faith for our souls wait on You to direct us. We hear from you and do what you say. We submit to You for You are our Rock of unyielding strength and our refuge is in You.
Psalm 62:5-8; Romans 8:14

52. We receive on behalf of our nation the answer to all its needs, because our God shall supply all our needs according to His riches in glory by Christ Jesus.
Philippians 4:19

53. Father, we ask Your help in understanding that for our nation to get out of the tremendous debt we're in, that each of us needs to learn how to be debt-free. I declare that You have given me the power to get wealth by Your covenant promise. I choose to renew my mind, and take the bondage off my thinking that says I can't live without debt. I choose to reprogram my soul with the belief that I can live debt-free by developing my faith for that (saying the scriptures below out loud). I receive Your grace and strength and give you glory as I resist the devil and You establish, strengthen, and settle me in this new belief system.[31]
Isaiah 41:10; 45:3; John 10:10; Philippians 4:19; James 4:7

54. For this cause we also, since the day we heard it, do not cease to pray for you, and to desire that you might be filled with the knowledge of His will in all wisdom and spiritual understanding.[32]
Colossians 1:9

55. I declare that I am humble enough to make the decisions that will allow me to pay off my credit card debt, car debt, mortgage, and all of my other indebtedness. I refuse to expect my fellow citizens to pay my debts, but instead I am self-sufficient as God intended. If that means I take my lunch to work rather than going out, I refuse to be too proud to do that and I do whatever it takes to get out of debt.

---

[31] It's a good idea to take the gospel as the last word. If we are tempted to doubt, let's DOUBT OUR OWN IDEAS before doubting God's.
[32] I am praying for you.

Day Seven

I place little value on the opinion of my peers but rather I value the opinion of God, my Maker, and my ultimate judge. I choose to plant the seeds of good so that I will live responsibly and have a harvest of good for my future.[33]
Proverbs 16:18; Psalm 10:3; 2 Corinthians 9:8; James 4:7

56. I trust in the Lord, and do good, so that I experience God's faithfulness. I delight myself in the Lord, and He gives me the desires of my heart. I unload every care on the Lord, and am confident in Him, knowing He will bring it to pass.
Psalm 37:4-5

57. I refuse to fret about wicked people who prosper at my expense, because they will soon be cut down like the grass. I refuse to be angry because it leads me to do evil as well. God has promised that those who do evil will be cut off, and be no more.
Psalm 37:1-2, 8-9

Your Notes:

---

[33] God resists the proud, but gives grace to the humble. Humble yourselves therefore under the mighty hand of God, that He may exalt you in due time, casting all your cares upon Him, for He cares for you. Be sober; be vigilant; because your adversary, the devil, walks about like a roaring lion, seeking whom he may devour. Resist him, steadfast in the faith, knowing that your brothers in the world experience the same sufferings. But may the God of all grace, who called us to His eternal glory by Christ Jesus, after you have suffered a while, perfect, establish, strengthen, and settle you. To Him be the glory and the dominion forever and ever. Amen. *1 Peter 5:5-10* (See also prayer #102 and its corresponding footnote on pg. 61 and the sidebar graphic on pg. 62).

The Lord says, "For as the heavens are higher than the earth, so are My ways higher than your ways, and My thoughts than your thoughts." *Isaiah 55:8-9*

Prayer For The Nation - Mary Ervasti

Your Notes:

Day VIII
Strength

58. No weapon formed against us will prosper and every tongue that rises against us in judgment we condemn. This is the heritage of the children of the Lord and our righteousness is of Him.
Isaiah 54:17

59. I declare that our armed forces are always well-protected, supplied with the right weaponry, and that no harm will come to them. I declare that those who have the responsibility for our military ensure that they are well equipped to defend themselves and us.
Judges 8:5-17

60. Father, we declare that any involvement in war is only according to Your perfect will. We declare that all of our troops remain in the Secret Place of the Most High and abide under the shadow of the Almighty. We ask for all wisdom for our President and our Congress for these decisions, we declare no troops are sent without the consent of the people through Congress and we loose ministering angels to make it so.
Psalm 91:1-16; 119:105; Hebrews 1:14; Job 22:28; James 1:5

61. We put You first in the concerns of our nation, Father God, and receive restoration. We accuse the devil – the thief – in the courts of heaven of all that he has stolen from our nation, and declare that he must restore to us double what he has taken.
Exodus 22:4, 7; John 10:10

62. As we anchor ourselves in You, our nation becomes anchored in You. Help us to get back to our roots so that it may again be said of us, that this is a nation that obeys the voice of the Lord their God, receives correction, and that the truth is known and spoken.
Jeremiah 7:28, 9:3; Psalm 64:3

63. We cheerfully do what the Lord requires of us - to do justly, to love mercy, and to walk humbly with our God.

Prayer For The Nation - Mary Ervasti

Micah 6:8

I sought for the key to the greatness and genius of America in her harbors; in her fertile fields and boundless forests; in her rich mines and vast world commerce; in her public school system and institutions of learning. I sought for it in her democratic Congress and in her matchless Constitution. Not until I went into the churches of America and heard her pulpits flame with righteousness did I understand the secret of her genius and power. America is great because America is good, and if America ever ceases to be good, America will cease to be great.

Alexis de Tocqueville

Your Notes:

Day IX
Mercy, vindication, corruption, joy

64. We are a chosen race, a royal priesthood, a dedicated nation, [God's] own purchased, special people, that we may set forth the wonderful deeds and display the virtues and perfections of Him who called us out of darkness into His marvelous light.
Exodus 19:5-6; 1 Peter 2:9

65. We ask You, Lord, for the mercy of showing us our sin, so that we can ask forgiveness, repent, receive the grace to change, and live in peace. Keep us from spiritual blindness.[34]
Zechariah 8:15-17; Job 5:17; Luke 11:4; Galatians 6:7;

66. I declare that every evil deed done against our nation is revealed so that people who are lawbreakers behind the scenes may be brought to justice, and those wrongfully accused may be vindicated. There is nothing hidden that won't be revealed, nor anything kept secret except that it may be known. What has been spoken in closets will be proclaimed upon the housetops.
Mark 4:22; Luke 12:3

67. I declare that all government officials taking bribes are exposed and brought to justice because surely oppression and extortion make a wise man foolish, and a bribe destroys the understanding and judgment. For God deliberately chose the foolish things of the world to put the wise to shame, and the weak to put the strong to shame.
Ecclesiastes 7:7; 1 Corinthians 1:27

68. I declare and decree that all of our leaders are just; ruling in the fear of God Who turns their hearts as He wills because they are in the hand of the Lord.
Job 22:8; 2 Samuel 23:3; Proverbs 21:1

69. We sing "Joy to the World, the Savior reigns" because He

---

[34] God presented Christ as a sacrifice of atonement through the shedding of his blood. He did this to demonstrate His righteousness, because in His forbearance He had not punished any of our unconfessed sins. *Romans 3:25*

Prayer For The Nation - Mary Ervasti

came to give us abundant life and the tools to defeat evil. Let heaven and nature sing, while fields and floods, rocks, hills and plains repeat the sounding joy.
Psalm 118:26; John 10:10; Luke 2:10-11; 19:40

70. Thank You, Lord, that because the Savior is born, sins and sorrows need no longer grow. When we accept Your salvation, it comes with the authority to overcome in this world. You came to make Your Blessings flow as far as the curse is found and we receive them.
Genesis 1:26; Deuteronomy 30:19; Proverbs 26:2; Luke 2:10-11; Romans 10:13

Your Notes:

Day X
Mighty men and women, led by the Spirit

71. We declare the steps of a good man/woman/child/nation are ordered by the Lord and we delight in His ways. Though we fall, we shall not be utterly cast down for the Lord upholds us with His hand.
Psalm 37:23-24

72. We declare that there are mighty men and women in this nation who stand up with the leaders who will take down the corruption in our government.
Job 22:8; Joshua 6:2; Ephesians 4:22; Romans 4:17

73. We declare that our people and our leaders honor the mighty men and women in our armed forces.
Job 22:8; Joshua 6:2; 2 Samuel 23:8-39; Romans 4:17

74. We humbly commit our righteous cause to the great Lord of the Universe who loves righteousness and hates iniquity.
Deuteronomy 8:18-20; Isaiah 23:11, 37:16; Daniel 2:21

75. Father, as I rest, let me be led by Your Spirit, because when the Spirit of truth comes, He guides me into all truth. He will not speak of Himself, but speak only what He hears, and He will show me things to come.
John 16:13; Hebrews 4:11; Romans 8:14

76. I am free of being puffed up with pride because with that comes emptiness, depression, and shame. Instead, I keep a humble attitude (like those who are lowly, who have been pruned and chiseled by trial, and have renounced self) and receive skillful and godly wisdom and soundness.[35]
Proverbs 11: 2

77. I put no trust in riches because they provide no security in

---

[35] "I think the most blessed thing in the world is to not get your way and be just as happy as you would have if you had gotten your way." *-Joyce Meyer*

Prayer For The Nation - Mary Ervasti

any day of wrath and judgment, but righteousness (uprightness and right standing with God) delivers me from death.
Proverbs 11:4

"In our lowest and most dangerous state, in 1776 and 1777, we sustained ourselves against the British Army of sixty thousand troops, commanded by...the ablest generals Britain could procure throughout Europe, with a naval force of twenty-two thousand seamen in above eighty men-of-war.

Who but a Washington, inspired by heaven, could have conceived the surprise move upon the enemy at Princeton—that Christmas Even when Washington and his army crossed the Delaware?

Who but the Ruler of the winds could have delayed the British reinforcements by three months of contrary ocean winds at a critical point of the war?

Or what but "a providential miracle? At the last minute detected the treacherous scheme of traitor Benedict Arnold, which would have delivered the American army, including George Washington himself, into the hands of the enemy?

On the French role in the Revolution, it is God who so ordered the balancing interests of nations as to reduce an irresistible motive in the European maritime powers to take our part...

The United States are under peculiar obligations to become a holy people unto the Lord our God."

Ezra Stiles, President of Yale College (1778-1795) before the governor and General Assembly of Connecticut in May 1783.
The American Patriot's Bible, p.1140

Day XI
*No worries, Integrity guides me,
Psalm 91 is for my protection*

78. I always act with integrity, and that guides me, because willfulness, contrariness, and crookedness would destroy me.
Proverbs 11:3

79. I refuse to be conformed to this world, but am transformed by the renewing of my mind, that I may prove what is the good, acceptable, and perfect will of God.
Romans 12:2

80. A false balance and unrighteous dealings are extremely offensive and shamefully sinful to the Lord; therefore, I treat people fairly because this is His delight.
Proverbs 11:1

81. I choose to be the light God has called me to be. I rest in the Lord, wait for Him, and patiently lean on Him because He has promised that I will receive all that's coming to me, including an abundance of peace.
Psalm 37:6-11

82. I declare that those who God desires to place into public office are placed in those offices by the votes of the people. These public officials dwell in the secret place of the Most High and remain stable and fixed under the shadow of the Almighty. God is their Refuge and Fortress, and they lean and rely on Him. They confidently trust Him. Therefore, He delivers them from every snare the devil sets for them and from every deadly disease. He covers them as they trust and find their refuge in Him. His Truth and Faithfulness shields them. They are free of the fear of terror or of the evil plots and slanders of wicked enemies. They refuse to fear pestilence, destruction, or sudden death. A thousand shots maybe taken at them – 10,000 at their right hand, but none shall overcome them as they witness the reward of the wicked from their secret place in God. Because they have made God their refuge and dwelling place, He gives His angels charge over

Prayer For The Nation - Mary Ervasti

them to accompany, defend, and preserve them in all their ways of obedience and service to Him. Because they love and honor God, He honors, delivers, and elevates them. Because they understand and expect to see His mercy, love, and kindness, God will never forsake them. They call and God answers and gives them long life as a bonus.[36]
Psalm 91

83. Thank you, Lord, that the angels of worship, the angels of war, the angel of the Lord and the Host of God are watching over our primaries, conventions, elections, and the counting of our votes. We declare all votes are counted and reported accurately, and any actions to the contrary are thwarted by Your angels.
Numbers 22:23-35; Job 22:28; Psalm 34:7; 35:4-6; 103:20; John 15:7

84. The Lord laughs at the wicked who plot against the righteous (those in right standing with God) in this nation; who plot against the poor and needy, to bring down the good, because He sees their own day of defeat coming. Their evil deeds will come back on them. This is God's Word, and I believe it.
Psalm 37:12-15; Galatians 6:7

Your Notes:

---

[36] Dear Prayer Partner: If this prayer causes you to choke a bit, please allow God to build your faith in it. This is the Word of God and a promise to us all who put our trust in Him. Faith comes by hearing and hearing by the Word of God. As you continue to give voice to it (I encourage you to say it out loud) the angels are going to hear and do as you say. This is the creative power of the Word of God. Didn't God say in Genesis, "Let there be light," and light was? Didn't Jesus say greater things than these will you do? Doesn't Hebrews say the Word of God is a sword capable of judging the heart? If we call ourselves believers, are we not to follow their example? Then as we say what God and Jesus have said, we will get the same results. We have their word on it. I'm praying for God's Holy boldness to come all over you.
Genesis 1:3; Psalm 103:20; John 14:12; Romans 10:17; Hebrews 1:14; 4:12,16

Day XII
Declaring things in advance as though they've occurred

85. Our Congressmen and Senators' steps are ordered by the Lord. Their decisions are in Your perfect will, in line with Your laws, and are for the benefit of the people. We call for more good men and women to represent us whose steps are ordered by the Lord.
Psalm 37:23

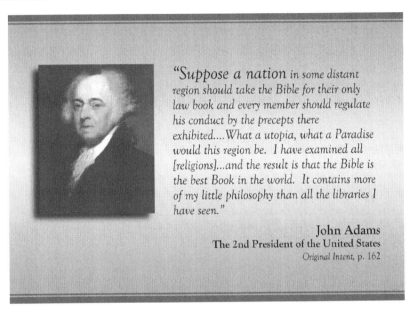

"*Suppose a nation* in some distant region should take the Bible for their only law book and every member should regulate his conduct by the precepts there exhibited....What a utopia, what a Paradise would this region be. I have examined all [religions]...and the result is that the Bible is the best Book in the world. It contains more of my little philosophy than all the libraries I have seen."

John Adams
The 2nd President of the United States
Original Intent, p. 162

86. Corrupt politicians in our nation are being cut off, but our citizens who do the right thing inherit our land.
Psalm 37:9,29

87. Blessed is the nation whose God is the Lord and whose people are counted among those whom He has chosen for His own inheritance.[37] We declare our nation is what God intends for us so that we

---
37 It is written in some of the books and diaries of the early immigrants to this nation that they were directed to come here by the word of the Lord in this scripture: "Now the Lord had said unto Abram, get thee out of thy country, and from thy kindred, and from thy father's house, unto a land that I will show thee: And I will make of thee a great nation, and I will bless thee, and make thy name great; and thou shalt be a blessing: And I will bless them that bless thee, and curse him that curses thee: and in thee shall all families of the earth be blessed."
Genesis 12:1-3

Prayer For The Nation - Mary Ervasti

are a blessing to the families of the earth.
Psalm 33:12

88. I declare America always stands with Israel. We pray for the peace of Jerusalem because all who love her will prosper. Let peace be within her walls and prosperity within her palaces because without Israel, we would not have the Word of God, which she preserved and handed down to us. We honor Israel with our gratitude.
Psalm 122:6-7; Matthew 18:19-20

89. Father God, I declare that our leaders practice Matthew 22:39 and love their neighbors as themselves. No longer do they love their power and privilege more than the people they represent. By honoring the people they represent, our leaders establish the vision of the people and exalt their vision rather than exalting themselves and robbing the people.
Daniel 11:14; Job 22:28

90. Father, help us understand the joy the Lord brought to the world with His coming. "Let every heart prepare Him room" so that we can experience the love and hope that is there for us. Let us receive Him as our King, understanding that the rise and fall of nations are in His hand.
Daniel 2:21; Luke 1:32

91. Lord, You are scattering the proud because they have followed the imagination of their hearts instead of listening to You and taking action on Your Word. Help me to hear You and do what you say.[38,39]
Psalm 119:9; John 10:27; Romans 8:13-14; 12:2-3

Israel was chosen by God to be His inheritance — to be the ones that He would give His bounty to. Through Christ, an Israelite, we are grafted into this family.
Romans 11; Galatians 3:16

38 The Virgin Mary said, "He has shown strength with His arm; he has scattered the proud in the imagination of their hearts." She believed and declared that the Lord brings the counsel of the heathen to nothing and makes the evil devices of people of no effect. His holy arm has won Him the victory: He has put down the mighty from their seats, and exalted them of low degree.
Luke 1:50-51; Psalm.33:10; 98:1

39 The Spirit Himself bears witness with my spirit. However, the voice of a stranger, I will not follow.
Jeremiah 7:23; John 10:4-5; Romans 8:16;

Day XIII
Yielding, repentance, new life

92. My soul magnifies the Lord (because I have asked him to live in me), and my spirit rejoices in God my Savior. He has regarded my low estate, and He that is mighty has done great things for me. Holy is His name![40]
Psalm 126:2-3; Job 5:11; Luke 1:46

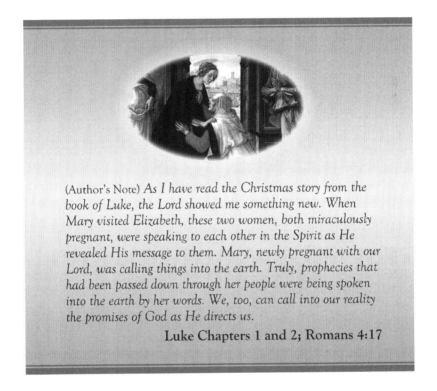

(Author's Note) *As I have read the Christmas story from the book of Luke, the Lord showed me something new. When Mary visited Elizabeth, these two women, both miraculously pregnant, were speaking to each other in the Spirit as He revealed His message to them. Mary, newly pregnant with our Lord, was calling things into the earth. Truly, prophecies that had been passed down through her people were being spoken into the earth by her words. We, too, can call into our reality the promises of God as He directs us.*
Luke Chapters 1 and 2; Romans 4:17

93. God's mercy is on my family and me because we reverence

---

[40] The Virgin Mary said, "My soul magnifies the Lord and my spirit has rejoiced in God my Savior (similar to what Hannah said declaring the works of the Lord in her own impossible conception). For he has regarded the low estate of his handmaiden for, behold, from henceforth all generations shall call me blessed. For He that is mighty hath done to me great things and holy is His name." She credits God's Word as the way to holiness.
Luke 1:48-49; 1 Samuel 2:1

Him and make Him our Lord.[41]
Genesis 17:7; Acts 10:34; Ephesians 2:12-13

94. I declare that our leaders make decisions to do good according to God's perfect will.[42]
Exodus 18:21; Deuteronomy 1:13; 16:18-19; Zechariah 7:9-10; James 4:17

95. Heavenly Father, we yield ourselves to You as Mary did, so that we may also receive the faith that you gave her. Since we are all created equal, and You are no respecter of persons, we have all been given the same measure of faith. Therefore, as we yield to You the same way she did, our faith can grow up in us just like Mary's.[43]
2 Chronicles 30:8; Acts 10:34; Romans 12:3

96. Father, we can see from your Word that we have become an idolatrous nation, making idols of money, power, and ourselves. How then shall we possess the land? Save us from the domination of those who would take away our freedoms. Save us from ourselves, and the habit of being so self-absorbed that we don't even see what we have become.
Ezekiel 33:25

97. Father, we repent from all our transgressions so that iniquity will not be our ruin. We cast away from us all the sins we have committed and ask You, Lord, for new hearts. Therefore we turn from death toward life. We confess our sin so that we receive the grace to do better. We yield to You and Your ways, and receive a heart that is in agreement with You, so that we may save our nation, possess the land, and prolong our days.
Ezekiel 18:30-32; Deuteronomy 5:33; 2 Chronicles 30:8; Romans 6:23; James 5:16

---

41 Mary said, "And His mercy is on them that fear him from generation to generation." She believed that the covenant God had made with Abraham also applied to her, and she declared that she was living proof.
Luke 1:50
42 Therefore to him that knows to do good, and does it not, to him it is sin.
James 4:17
43 Mary said, "He has filled the hungry with good things; and the rich he hath sent away empty. He has helped his servant Israel, in remembrance of His mercy He spoke to our fathers, to Abraham, and to his seed forever." Mary declared the words of God to Abraham, who had a child by faith also, and spoke of the covenant in the past tense, as though it had already happened.
Psalm 71:19; 98:3; Galatians 3:16

Day Thirteen

98. Thank You, Father, that You are no respecter of persons, (all are equal in the eyes of God) and that You have created us all in Your image, and given each of us the same measure of faith to pursue our God-given aspirations and dreams.
Genesis 1:27; Acts 10:34; Romans 12:3

Your Notes:

Prayer For The Nation - *Mary Ervasti*

Your Notes:

Day XIV
Prepared path, taking responsibility

99. I declare we listen to how You want things done, Lord, because You know the path You have prepared for us. We refuse to go our own way and leave ourselves with nothing to depend on but our own intellect. We tap into Your infinite knowledge and understanding saying, "Except the Lord builds the house, we labor in vain who build it; except the Lord keeps the city, the watchman wakes in vain."[44]
Psalm 127:1; Joshua 1:7; Romans 8:14

100. I take personal responsibility for the freedom I've been given, and think of the benefit of all rather than just the benefit of my family and myself. What I do matters beyond myself.
Matthew 7:12

101. I lean on You, Lord and listen to and trust You for the protection of our nation, so that I know from You what is my part to do.
Proverbs 3:5; Romans 8:14

102. I choose to be steadfast in confessing Your Word before You, Lord, by saying, "I declare that all things are possible to me as I listen to my Lord Jesus Christ. I hear Him; I yield myself to Him in every situation so that I am at the right place, at the right time, doing the right thing, for the right reasons."[45]

---

[44] Just because we see trouble, doesn't mean we can do anything about it on our own without God.

[45] Jesus was training the generals (the disciples) in Matthew, and he modeled this discipline before them (*see* Matthew 14). I believe faith for the impossible (believing that all things are possible as Jesus believed His Father) drove him to bless the five loaves and two fish, and believe that they would feed five thousand men plus the women and children. I believe faith for the impossible kept Him tuned into His Father after He sent them all away and just wanted to sit and remember John.

He heard His Father's call to get up and rescue his disciples. I believe faith for the impossible caused Him to say to Himself, "It's the middle of the night. I can't go get a boat, but they need Me now." He walked on the water to save them. I believe faith for the impossible caused Peter to challenge Jesus as to who He was, and to walk on the water himself when Jesus called him to come. Then doubt caused him to sink until the Lord caught him.

The twelve disciples were a ragtag group by various estimations. However, the scripture says if any man lacks wisdom, let him ask of God and He will give it liberally if we ask in faith.

Prayer For The Nation - Mary Ervasti

John 10:14-16; Matthew 19:26; Romans 10:10

We live in a time when we, the body of Christ, need to be doing the impossible. We can do the impossible as we discipline ourselves to be the army of God under the explicit orders of our Commander, the Lord Jesus Christ.

103. We receive the wisdom to understand the truth of Your Word, Lord. Without You we can do nothing, but abiding in You, we bring forth much fruit.
John 15:5

104. Jesus, You said the thief comes to steal, and to kill, and to destroy, and that You came that we might have life, and that we might have it more abundantly. Therefore, today we stand before You in the spirit, fighting against the principalities and powers that have come against our nation. These principalities and powers will never separate us from Your love, because Your love never fails. Nor will they steal, kill or destroy the American dream of life, liberty, and the pursuit of happiness because we stand and do Your bidding as our

---

(con't from p. 59) These disciples watched Jesus and believed. In doing so, they proved that the wisdom of this world is foolishness with God and the way of the Lord makes the simple wise.
James 1:5; 1 Corinthians 3:19

Day Fourteen

founders did in our beginnings.
John 10:10; Romans 8:37-39; Ephesians 6:12; 1 Corinthians 13:8

105. We declare and decree that our government is made up of wise people, understanding, and known among us as good and worthy to represent us. We ask that You, Lord, remove any wicked from among them so the righteous inherit this land.
Deuteronomy 1:13; Psalm 37:35-36, 29; Job 22:28

Your Notes:

Prayer For The Nation - Mary Ervasti

Your Notes:

Day XV
What's right, strength, trust in God

106. Father, help us to be righteous (doing the right thing, at the right time for the right reasons with the right people), so that our nation is exalted because we hear You and do what You say.[46]
Proverbs 14:34

107. We refuse to look to man for what we should do, or to the social norms, or what others expect of us in our station in life, but we ask God for wisdom, because He has promised to give it to all men liberally. We ask in faith, not wavering. Thank you, Lord, that we are blessed when we endure temptation: for when we are tried, we shall receive the crown of life, which the Lord has promised to us that love him.
James 1:5-6, 12

108. Because we trust You, Lord, we can do what needs to be done in our nation. Because we come to You with the right attitudes and motives, we can have a godly nation. Because we believe that You are a rewarder of those who diligently seek You, we have the power to act in a righteous manner, and in so doing, lift up our nation.
Mark 11:22; Matthew 6:5-15; 7:7-11; Philippians 4:5-6; Hebrews 11:6

109. Lord, judge the people: judge me, oh Lord, according to my righteousness, and according to the integrity that is in me. Let the violence of the wicked come to an end; but establish the just. God, create in me a clean heart and renew a right spirit within me.

---

[46] What do we do when we realize that the "ME" generation of the 1960s has evolved into a culture of people that think about ourselves more than anyone else? I will admit it is a temptation that I have fought regularly, and that I am committed to eradicating. This seed was planted in our nation with the first settlers who came to Virginia who were looking for gold. However, because they didn't all pitch in and help each other, most of them died. (See *The Light and the Glory* 1977 p. 108-136)

However, God, being faithful, planted another seed in our nation with the Mayflower Company who had been schooled in selflessness and the word of God for several years in the Netherlands after leaving England to seek religious freedom. In the Netherlands they couldn't find work, and had to depend upon and help each other in order to survive--good preparation for settling an unknown land that would require the same. (See *The Light and the Glory* p. 85)

Prayer For The Nation - Mary Ervasti

Psalm 7:8-9; 51:10

110. We are the redeemed of the Lord whom he has redeemed from the hand of the enemy.
Isaiah 51:11; Psalm 107:2

111. Father, help us to be strong in You, and in the power of Your might. We put on Your whole armor that we may be able to stand against the wiles of the devil. We put on Your whole armor, and we stand our ground until Your deliverance comes. We stand firm with the belt of truth buckled around our waist, with the breastplate of righteousness in place, and with our feet fitted with the readiness that comes from the gospel of peace. We take the shield of our faith, and quench all the fiery darts of the wicked. We take the helmet of salvation, and the sword of the Spirit, which is the word of God, praying always for all the saints.[47]
Ephesians 6:10-18; 1 Timothy 2:1-2

112. Father, have mercy on us. Forgive us for allowing ourselves to be tempted and led away by our own undisciplined, unwise desires for more. Let us instead be led by Your Holy Spirit, manifesting Your perfect will in the earth.
James 1:14; John 14:26; Romans 8:14

Your Notes:

---

[47] Saints are those who bless the Lord, who praise Him, sing in their beds, speak the word of God as a sword, act in faith, pray, give thanks for God's holiness, love the Lord, fear/reverence Him, and shout with joy.
Psalm 148:14; 149:5-6; Romans 10:9; 1 Corinthians 1:2,30; Hebrews 4:12; Jude 1:3; Revelation 5:8

Day XVI
Labor, rest, clarity, giving, God's faithfulness

113. We labor and then enter into rest.[48] We have been laboring in our prayers for our nation, and we have made progress. We have had a change of heart in some areas, and we continue to press on. Lord, help us to rest when we need it.
Hebrews 4:11

114. Father, we ask Your forgiveness for the sin of silent resignation and conformity to today's social norms that we know are not godly. We humble ourselves before You and confess that we kept silent when we saw our society going down the wrong path. In keeping silent, we emboldened the rebellious who have put their sin in Your face, and called it good. We pray now and seek Your face and Your ways. We turn from our disobedience and our wicked ways. Help us in every way to be faithful to Your ways. Give us wisdom, understanding, and knowledge of Your ways.
2 Chronicles 7:14; Deuteronomy 7:9; John 14:6

115. I give as the Lord shows me to give without compromise knowing that whatever He says to give He intends to multiply back to me. I give liberally because I have more than enough.
Proverbs 19:17; Luke 6:38; John 10:10; Philippians 4:19; Romans 8:14

116. I declare I am strong in You, Lord, and in the power of Your might. I choose to be led by the Holy Spirit, so that I can truly be a son/daughter/child of God, knowing that I am in Your will, and that You are directing my path. I listen for You, so that You can author my prayers and grow my faith to bring them to pass. I refuse to think up my own ideas and then try to put Your name on them.
Ephesians 6:10; Romans 8:14; Hebrews 12:2

117. Father, You said that if we humble ourselves, seek You, turn from our wicked ways, and pray, You would hear from heaven

---

[48] Too much work can cause stress. Too much stress can cause us to react rather than respond in faith. We need our Sabbath rests (no matter what day we take them) in order to keep our faith stabilized.

forgive our sin, and heal our land. I believe and I receive it, Lord. I choose to continue to seek You and believe until it happens. I choose to continue to humble myself, confess my sins, and turn from my wicked ways.
2 Chronicles 7:14

Healing Our Land

"If my people, which are called by my name, shall humble themselves, and pray, and seek my face, and turn from their wicked ways; then will I hear from heaven, and will forgive their sin, and will heal their land."

2 Chronicles 7:14

118. Father, thank You that I hear clearly what You are saying to me because I desire to do my part for our nation. It's no mistake that I am living at this time. I have come to the kingdom for such a time as this.
Esther 4:14; Romans 8:14

119. We dedicate our education system, our nation, and our government to God. We declare that Americans raise up godly citizens and leaders. We declare that all educators teach the fundamentals that will once again put our nation at the top in the world, not because we measure ourselves against the world's standards, but against God's standards of excellence.
Exodus 18:21-22; Deuteronomy 1:13, 16-17; 6:6-8; 16:18-19, 25:1, 27:19; Zechariah 7:9-10; Joshua 1:7-8

Day Sixteen

120. Father, Your Word says that You will never leave us or forsake us. That means that once we obey Your Word and act in faith, You will not desert us, but You will help us to accomplish Your purposes. You have promised to be the author and finisher of our faith. We take You at Your Word, and we believe it![49]
Hebrews 13:5, 12:2

121. By the mercies of God, we present our bodies a living sacrifice, holy, acceptable unto God, which is our reasonable service.
Romans 12:1

Your Notes:

---

[49] But he who does the truth comes to the light, that his deeds may be clearly seen, that they have been done in God.
John 3:21
Now more than ever, we need truth and light in our everyday dealings and in our nation. Let us plant a seed of truth in our day-to-day dealings so that it will grow up and take firm root in our nation. Let us, as individuals, be as true as we expect our elected officials to be. They are only a clear reflection of what we have become. Let us believe that the former and the latter rain will come this week, and we will have a harvest on our prayers. Impossible you say? We serve the God of the impossible, and we need to start understanding that He knows more than we could begin to fathom.
Jesus beheld them, and said, "With men this is impossible; but with God all things are possible."
Matthew 19:26; Ezekiel 36:26; Isaiah 33:22

Prayer For The Nation - Mary Ervasti

Your Notes:

Day XVII
Not to worry, integrity, confidence, housecleaning, Israel

122. Father, we ask Your forgiveness once again for allowing things to get so far out of control. We refuse, resist, reject, and rebuke all worry, but in everything by prayer and supplication with thanksgiving let our requests be made known unto You. And Your peace, which passes all understanding, keeps our hearts and minds through Christ Jesus.
Isaiah 43:5; James 4:7; Philippians 4:6-8

123. We refuse to make higher education, greed, and advancement of self our gods. Instead, we advance our neighbors by doing good for the benefit of all rather than for a line on our resume and the advancement of self.[50]
Luke 6:38; John 13:34; 2 Timothy 3:1-5

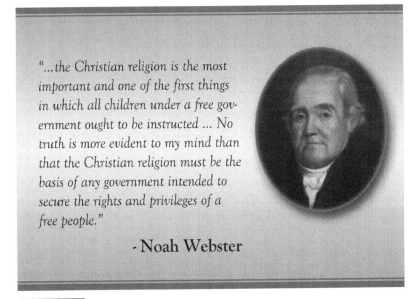

"...the Christian religion is the most important and one of the first things in which all children under a free government ought to be instructed ... No truth is more evident to my mind than that the Christian religion must be the basis of any government intended to secure the rights and privileges of a free people."

- Noah Webster

---

50 John Dewey said, "There is no God, and there is no soul. Hence, there are no needs for the props of traditional religion." John Dewey was a founding member of the American Civil Liberties Union, an early member of the Socialist Party of America, and a member of the Progressive Party. He died in 1952.

Those "props of traditional religion" have been largely eroded in our nation, and our society has ceased to be the godly nation that made us great. It's up to us to turn back to God, to ask him what to do, and to begin the change *in ourselves.*

Prayer For The Nation - Mary Ervasti

124. Father, we ask You for the former and latter rain for these seeds of transparency, integrity, honesty, and truth that we are planting now in our own lives. We declare these seeds will grow up and produce a harvest in our citizens; and, therefore, our education system, our businesses, and our government. We commit to living this way, and ask that You help us to change. In doing so we change our nation to one whose people are honest, truthful, and walk in integrity.
Deuteronomy 11:14; John 14:10

125. I refuse to trust in man or believe in human strength more than God's strength, because the Lord says the man who wants nothing to do with the Lord is cursed. He's like a shrub or a person who is naked and destitute in the desert. He doesn't see when good comes because he's not getting those signals from the Lord. I am blessed because I trust in the Lord, and count Him as my hope and confidence. I am like a tree planted by the waters whose roots go down to the river. When the heat comes, her leaf is green and has no anxiety in the drought because she still produces fruit.
Jeremiah 17:5-8

126. We declare the people of this nation are heard, first by God and then by our leaders. We ask You, God, for new hearts that are soft toward You, and to be free of the stony hearts that wanted our own way. We declare that as we yield to You and do as You say that You move on our leaders. We declare that Your Word, Father, is a lamp unto our feet and a light unto our path. It makes the way clear for us – we see it, and do what You show us to do. We declare that You sanctify us with Your Word of Truth.
Ezekiel 36:26; Psalm 119:105; John 17:17

127. Father, please clean out of me everything that would stand in the way of my doing Your perfect will. Put me in spiritual boot camp now, so that when the battle rages around me, I will be practiced at hearing from You and KNOWING what to do. Create in me a clean heart, oh God and renew a right spirit within me. I believe that as I trust You, doubts fall away, and I stand unwavering when evil comes.
Psalm 51:10; Ephesians 6:13

Day Seventeen

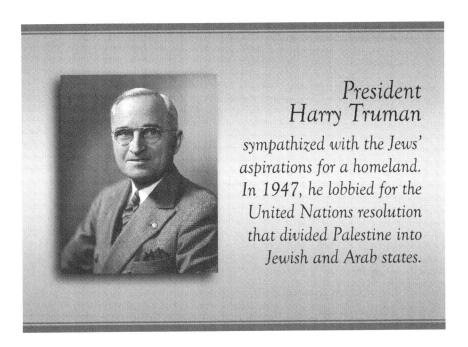

President Harry Truman *sympathized with the Jews' aspirations for a homeland. In 1947, he lobbied for the United Nations resolution that divided Palestine into Jewish and Arab states.*

128. Lord God, I bless Israel, and I pray for the peace of Jerusalem.[51] Let them receive the rewards of bringing us the gospel of Jesus Christ by which we are saved, and by which we can walk in all the promises that You have for us. Father, I declare that our nation blesses Israel and speaks in her defense in obedience to God's Word. We need Your blessings now in this time of challenges in our nation.
Genesis 12:3; Deuteronomy 32:49; Joshua 14:1; 16:15; 21:43; 23:8; Psalm 122:6

---

51 American foreign service experts strongly opposed the creation of a Jewish state in Palestine, warning that Arab countries would cut off oil and unite to destroy the Jews. Truman's wife, Margaret, said that was the most difficult decision her husband faced as President, but Truman held firm despite the heated opposition. On May 14, 1948, David Ben-Gurion read a declaration of Jewish independence, establishing the state of Israel. At midnight, the British rule over Palestine ended and 11 minutes later, the White House recognized the state of Israel. The Chief Rabbi in Israel, Isaac Halevi Herzog, later told Truman, "God put you in your mother's womb so that you would be the instrument to bring about Israel's rebirth after 2000 years." Psalm 137 was Truman's favorite according to Dr. Richard G. Lee, General Editor of *The American Patriot's Bible*.

Prayer For The Nation - Mary Ervasti

Your Notes:

Day XVIII
Cheating, approval, submission, life and death

129. Lord, we ask forgiveness for all the times that we have lied, cheated, manipulated, hidden our lies, and covered our dishonesty. We confess these things as sin, and recognize we are part of what's wrong with our nation. We receive Your forgiveness and grace to do the right things, at the right time, for the right reasons so that we never fear the light of Truth. We thank You for Your promise that, when we confess our sins, they are as far as the East is from the West. I declare that our citizens and all in government hear from the Spirit of Truth. We declare the devil is bound, and give him no place to deceive this nation. We refuse to cast away our confidence in God and His Word to give us the miracle of restoration.
Joel 2:23; Psalm 103:12; 1 Thessalonians 5:1-6; John 2:20; 16:13; Revelation 20:2-3; Hebrews 10:35

130. I hear the Holy Spirit and I know and obey His voice. He speaks through my spirit, but the voice of a stranger, I refuse to follow. Therefore, things go well for me.
Jeremiah 7:23; John 10:4-5; Romans 8:14

131. Father, root out of us the need to be accepted by and approved of by others, socially acceptable, and politically correct, and replace that need with the determination to be completely obedient to You. We declare the eyes of our understanding are enlightened, that we walk worthy of You, that we do good, we are just, we love mercy, and we walk humbly before You.[52]
Micah 6:8; Ephesians 1:18; 1 Thessalonians 2:12; Hebrews 13:21; 2 Peter 1:3

132. I commit myself to meditate on Your Word day and night, that I may observe to do according to all that is written in it. For then my way is prosperous, and then I have good success.
Joshua 1:8

---

52 The Catholic Church has a ceremony on Ash Wednesday during which they trace a cross on everyone's forehead with ashes. That's to remind us that we are made of dust. But for the grace of God that is all we are. To obey the God Who has allowed those who come to Him to share in the riches of the glory of His inheritance, requires a humble, submissive spirit that yields to Him in everything.
Romans 12:3; 2 Chronicles 30:8

Prayer For The Nation - Mary Ervasti

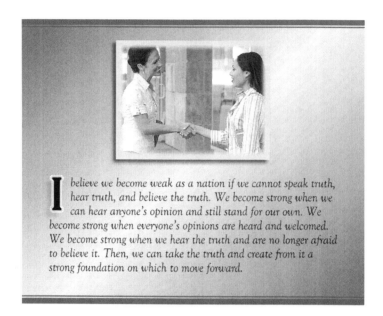

I believe we become weak as a nation if we cannot speak truth, hear truth, and believe the truth. We become strong when we can hear anyone's opinion and still stand for our own. We become strong when everyone's opinions are heard and welcomed. We become strong when we hear the truth and are no longer afraid to believe it. Then, we can take the truth and create from it a strong foundation on which to move forward.

133. I choose to submit myself to the good elders around me. I learn from their mistakes and their knowledge of history. I choose to be subject to the wise ones around me, and be clothed with humility because You, God, resist the proud and give grace to the humble. I choose to humble myself, therefore, under Your mighty hand that You may promote me in due time, casting all my care upon You, for You care for me.
1 Peter 5:5-7

134. He that works deceit shall not dwell within my house. He who tells lies shall not continue in my presence.[53]
Psalm 101:7

135. Father, You, have set before us life and death, blessings and curses. We choose life in You and Your perfect will. You have come that we might have life more abundantly. You are the Way, the Truth,

---

53 **The Whole Truth**
Truth must prevail in our households, on our tax returns (even if we don't like the way the government is spending our money), and in the way we do business before we can point fingers at anyone who we believe to be deceitful. We need to humble ourselves under the mighty hand of God, that He may exalt us in due time, casting all our cares upon Him, for He cares for us and because God resists the proud, but gives grace to the humble. We need all the grace we can get.
1 Peter 5:5-7

Day Eighteen

and the Life, and You said our ears would hear a word behind us, saying, "This is the way, walk in it." We trust that we hear You in this, Lord, because You are faithful!
Deuteronomy 7:9; 30:19; Isaiah 30:21; John 10:10; 14:6

Your Notes:

Prayer For The Nation - *Mary Ervasti*

Your Notes:

Day XIX
Idols, rooted and grounded, wisdom, no condemnation

136. Lord, I ask forgiveness for all the idols of family, media, education, business, government, arts, entertainment, even religion that I have worshipped instead of worshipping You. I put these idols down now. I trusted in them instead of You and they are unworthy. I have heard You and have returned to You. Thank You that the false kings of these idols are falling according to Your Word.
Hosea 8:4,6; 10-14; 11:7-12; 14:1-9

137. I choose to grow, being rooted and grounded in God's love, comprehending what is the breadth, length, depth, and height of the love of Christ, which passes knowledge, that I might be filled with all the fullness of God.
Ephesians 3:17-19

138. Father, we humbly submit ourselves to You, submitting our own ideas to Yours because Your thoughts are higher than our thoughts. Help us to be free of pride and arrogance so that we are free of thinking our ideas are better than Yours (You who know all!). In doing this, we receive the grace of humility, and all Your guidance, Lord. We ask Your forgiveness for all the times that we have gone our own way rather than asking for Your plan. Thank You for showing us the way.
Isaiah 55:9; John 14:6

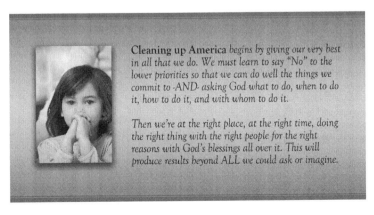

Cleaning up America *begins by giving our very best in all that we do. We must learn to say "No" to the lower priorities so that we can do well the things we commit to -AND- asking God what to do, when to do it, how to do it, and with whom to do it.*

Then we're at the right place, at the right time, doing the right thing with the right people for the right reasons with God's blessings all over it. This will produce results beyond ALL we could ask or imagine.

139. Lord, I expect that as I plant seeds of honesty and integrity, I will have a harvest of the same coming back to me. I ask Your forgiveness for all the times that I have not told the truth, and ask for Your grace to do better. Lord, I ask for your mercy on me and on my nation.
Mark 4:26-29

140. Lord, I promise to direct my children and my household to keep Your ways by doing what is right and just, so that by pleasing You, we will inherit the promise of Abraham.[54]
Genesis 17 and 18; 19:1-29; 13:2; 21:1-8

141. I receive wisdom about taking my nation back to a godly standard for the benefit of all.
Proverbs 4:7; Ephesians 4:3, 13

142. I choose to get into the habit of examining myself, knowing that God won't condemn me, but that He will lovingly convict me of my wrongdoing. Lord, You have promised to forgive me if I ask, so help me to examine myself and my sins without any shame. Then, when I ask, You will show me how to do it the right way. Help me to become selfless and to avoid the pitfalls of selfishness for myself, my family, my community, my state, and my nation.
Proverbs 16:18; Psalm 26:2; 78:38; 1 Corinthians 11:28; 2 Corinthians 13:5; Luke 23:34; James 5:15; Ephesians 4:32

---

54 **It's A Family Affair**
   In every strong family, there are standards and rules that are required of everyone. For example – there shall be no lying, no cheating, no stealing, or acting as if we are just so much more special than the others. In keeping a standard, we come together in strength. However, if the standard is violated, and no consequences are brought to bear, good behavior and strength declines. *Proverbs 6:20;*
   When things fall apart, God's people need to re-establish high standards and enforce them for the good of all. Babylon fell apart because of its self-indulgence. So it is with a nation when the people ignore the law, the government is lax in enforcing it, or binds the people under too many laws and regulations. Things begin to break down and fall apart. *Jeremiah 50:1-2; Revelation 14:8, 16:19, 18:21-24*
   In either scenario, when the leaders stand and enforce or correct the laws again, those who have been getting by with lying, cheating, and stealing are going to be unhappy. They may resort to blaming and violent expressions. However, the Lord is on the side of the just. Justice upholds the law.
Deuteronomy 1:16; 16:18-19; 25:1; 27:19; Zechariah 7:9-10

Day XX
Casting cares, undaunted, standing up, your voice

143. I daily examine myself against the word of God to see if I have thought more about myself than I've thought about God and others; if I have lied to others or about others; if I have committed any sin; if I have refused to forgive others; or neglected to confess my sins and ask forgiveness. Then I ask God to forgive me and give me the grace to improve.
James 5:16; Matthew 18:21, 22; Ephesians 1:7

144. I humble myself under Your mighty hand, Father, believing in Your Word, and knowing it is higher than my thoughts. I choose to cast my cares on You because You care for me. I believe that I can do the impossible with Your help. If you say, "owe no man," then I'm going to put my faith in Your Word and believe that as I meditate on it, say it, and listen for Your insights, concepts and ideas, I will hear them, carry them out, and become debt-free. When the devil says, "Who are you kidding? You will never get out of debt!" I will resist him, call him the liar that he is, and say, "With men this is impossible; but with God all things are possible, and God is with me in this!"[55]
2 Kings 4:1-7; John 8:44; Matthew 17:20, 24-27

145. We are undaunted by the magnitude of problems in our nation and in our lives because we remember that the Angel of the Lord, the angels of Worship, the angels of War and the Host of God have been assigned to help us. Our continued declarations of faith keeps them working on our behalf as we run with patience the race set before us, looking unto Jesus, the author and finisher of our faith.
Hebrews 12:1-2; Psalm 103:20

146. Father, we declare in faith that we, the people, stand up for the rule of law. We refuse to let the liars, the cheaters, the thieves, and self-interested people rule in our nation.[56]

---

55 You, Lord, will keep him in perfect peace, whose mind is stayed on Thee: because he trusts in Thee.
Isaiah 26:3
56 In the book of Proverbs, it says "These six things doth the Lord hate; yea, seven are an

Prayer For The Nation - Mary Ervasti

Proverbs 6:16-19; Joshua 1:7-8

When Jesus heard that his cousin and partner in the faith, John, had been beheaded, he went to the desert to be alone. However, the people followed him, and He had compassion on them, healed their sick, and fed them. That takes discipline when you are grieving. Jesus would likely have been taunted by the devil with evil thoughts regarding those who killed John. He could have spewed His rage all over everyone, but I believe He commanded His flesh to submit to His spirit (something any of us can do in His name), and He acted in love. He recognized that the evil spirits at work with the people who killed John were sent from the devil; and the best way to get back at the devil was to heal the sick, and to demonstrate faith for the impossible.

Ephesians 6:12
Matthew 19:26

---

abomination unto him. A proud look, a lying tongue, and hands that shed innocent blood, a heart that devises wicked imaginations, feet that are swift in running to mischief, a false witness that speaks lies, and he that sows discord among his brethren." *Proverbs 6:16-19*

In the book of Romans, it says "For to be carnally minded is death; but to be spiritually minded is life and peace." To be carnally minded is to think about what we can see, feel, taste, touch, smell - the physical senses. If we are led by our carnal selves, we will surely get into trouble. *Romans 8:6,14*

Day Twenty

The only reason God set up a system of laws was so that people would get along together peacefully, living life to the fullest, and by doing so, positioning themselves to be recipients of His blessings and promises. The act of not obeying these laws is called **sin**. In the book of James, it says, "Then when lust hath conceived, it brings forth sin; and sin, when it is finished, brings forth death." (Lust means to strongly desire or covet [want ardently something that belongs to someone else].)

James 1:15
Proverbs 10:3

147. When our cause is right, good, and unselfish, we have all of heaven behind us. Jesus is interceding at the right hand of God for us, and if God is for us, who can be against us?
Romans 8:14,31,34

148. Help me to make my voice heard. I declare that You put Your words in my mouth, Lord. I declare that the body of Christ comes together in unity to rule and reign according to Your plan.
Psalm 49:3; 119:99; Proverbs 4:7; Ephesians 4:3, 13

149. We are troubled on every side, yet not distressed; we are perplexed but not in despair; persecuted, but not forsaken, cast down,

but not destroyed. Even in this, our selfishness, pride, unforgiveness, and sin of every kind is dying within us as we accept Christ into

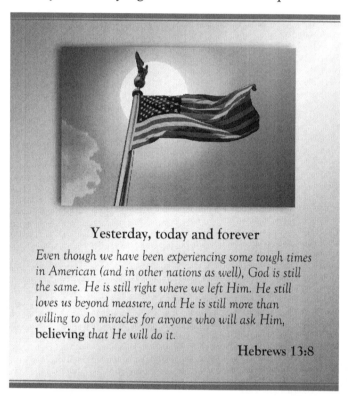

Yesterday, today and forever

Even though we have been experiencing some tough times in American (and in other nations as well), God is still the same. He is still right where we left Him. He still loves us beyond measure, and He is still more than willing to do miracles for anyone who will ask Him, **believing** *that He will do it.*

Hebrews 13:8

every inch of us so that He can work through us to stand, fight, and take our victory. We believe, therefore we speak; knowing that He that raised up Christ, shall raise us up also by our faith in Him.
Psalm 2; 3:5-8; Isaiah 41:10; 2 Corinthians 4:8-13

Your Notes:

Day XXI
Same measure of faith, seek first the Kingdom

150. Father, you have given each of us the same measure of faith, so if some can live selflessly, so can I. It's only a question of developing my faith just like I would develop a muscle. Help me to stretch my faith further expecting more and more seemingly impossible things to happen in my life. Help me to trust You, whose thoughts are higher than any of my thoughts. Thank You for helping me, Lord.[57]
Isaiah 55:9; Matthew 19:26; Romans 12:3

151. In obedience to Your Word, Lord, we take no thought for what we shall eat, drink, and how we will be clothed. For You, heavenly Father, know that we have need of all these things, but because we seek *first* Your kingdom and Your righteousness, all these things are added unto us.
Matthew 6:31-33

152. I owe no man anything, but to love him for he that loves another has fulfilled the law. Therefore, I commit to getting out of debt and staying out of debt so that God can direct me to give and do according to His perfect will without any debt to stand in my way.
Exodus 22:25; Deuteronomy 15:6; Romans 13:8

153. Father, thank You that You are saving us from government intrusion in our lives. Thank You that You have redeemed us to a land of freedom where reasonable men and women may lead quiet

---

57 **A Thousand People In The Street**
  As we look at the situation in the world today, we see nations falling under the weight of their entitlement programs, and the people rioting in the streets because of what they want for themselves. We need to heed the practices of the Puritans who, schooled in constant self-examination, founded our nation. In reading their journals, we can see that self-examination is what they did at the end of every day. They were practiced in self-denial, self-reliance, examining themselves to see to it that they were unselfish, thinking of the benefit of all, and measuring themselves against the principles of the Bible. This is the foundation on which our nation was built, and this is our reasonable service today. Now is the time to take responsibility for ourselves, not looking to men to take care of us when God has promised to supply all our needs according to His riches in Glory by Christ Jesus.
  Romans 12:1; Philippians 4:19

and peaceable lives in all godliness and honesty. Thank You that we can make our voices heard, as we choose to participate in the ruling of our nation. Thank You that we are a government of the people, by the people, and for the people.
1 Timothy 2:1-2; Romans 4:17

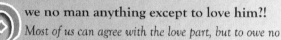 we no man anything except to love him?!

Most of us can agree with the love part, but to owe no man? That seems, to many of us, to be the impossible dream. However, paying cash as we go is not so much about having enough money to do this, but deciding to obey God's Word. As we believe and declare that we have the money according to God's Word, it gives us the power to do it, because faith comes by hearing the Word of God, confession is made unto salvation (even salvation from debt) and faith is the substance of things hoped for, the evidence of things not seen. This gives Him glory and pleases Him. He is a very loving Father, and wants to help us and to prosper us. Let's look at just a few of His words about it:

"And you shall remember the Lord your God, for it is He who gives you power to get wealth that He may establish His covenant which He swore to your fathers, as it is this day."

Deuteronomy 8:18

"Beloved, I wish above all things that you may prosper and be in health, even as your soul prospers."

3 John 1:2

"But Jesus beheld them, and said unto them, 'With men this is impossible; but with God all things are possible."

Matthew 19:26

Christ who healed the sick, raised the dead, and died on the cross for us said, "Greater things than these will you do." That's impossible to the mind, so we need to do these things in faith by the power of the Holy Spirit. Don't ever ask your mind if you can do what God tells you to do–especially the greater things. That's a mind bender because the mind is finite, and the Spirit is infinite. This is why when God said He made us in His image; He made us with a spirit. That's the God part, and the only part that can handle the impossible.

Hebrews 11:1; Exodus 34:6-7; Galatians 5:16; 1 Peter 4:6; Romans 10:17; Matthew 26:41; John 3:6; Romans 8:1-5; 4:17; Galatians 5:16; Philippians 4:19

Day Twenty-One

154. My God supplies all my needs according to his riches in glory by Christ Jesus.
Philippians 4:19

155. I refuse to be stiff-necked and rebellious, which stops the flow of God's blessings to me in the land of milk and honey. I refuse to think too highly of myself because that only ends in destruction. Instead, I yield to God and follow the Holy Spirit without fear or hesitation.
Exodus 33:3; Proverbs 16:18; Romans 12:3

156. Thank you, Lord, that when we confess our sins You remove them as far as the East is from the West.
Psalm 103:12; 1 John 1:9

157. Our nation knows the Word of God, our spiritual weapons of warfare, how to use them, and how to live in God's Kingdom principles. Therefore, using these, we overcome the works of the devil.
Job 22:28; 2 Corinthians 6:7; 10:4-5; Ephesians 6:10-18; Revelation 12:11

Your Notes:

Prayer For The Nation - *Mary Ervasti*

Your Notes:

Day XXII
Grace and mercy, terrorists, negative passions

158. Thank You, Lord, for the grace and mercy to examine ourselves and spend time with You daily, so that we can see opportunities when You put them in front of us.
Psalm 26:2; 1 Corinthians 11:28; 2 Corinthians 13:5; 1 Timothy 1:2;

159. Lord, you have shown us in prayer that we in the United States have been like the children of Israel, spoken of in Nehemiah. They had turned away from their godly beginnings, and become hard-hearted and stiff-necked toward God. You have given us the land that flows with milk and honey, and we have squandered it. Since turning away from You and Your ways we have become weak and easily plundered by outsiders who have sent their evil doers into our land. They take advantage of crisis, and even create crisis. Because we have not been looking to You, we haven't even seen how vulnerable we are. We have lost the wisdom that comes from Your Word to us in the Bible. Now, however, we are looking to You and gaining wisdom to take our nation back to its godly beginnings.
Psalm 26:2; 1 Timothy 1:2; 1 Corinthians 11:28; 2 Corinthians 13:5;

160. I bind the devil from bringing terrorists to this nation and plead the blood of Jesus Christ against them. I declare any attempts by terrorists to enter this nation are exposed and thwarted. I loose ministering angels in heaven and in earth, past, present, and future to make it so.
Matthew 16:19; John 15:7

161. I sing of mercy and loving-kindness and justice to You, O Lord. I will behave myself wisely and give heed to the blameless way. I walk within my house in integrity and with a blameless heart. I set no base or wicked thing before my eyes. I hate the work of them who turn aside [from the right path]; it shall not grasp hold of me. A perverse heart departs from me, and I will know no evil person or thing. I refuse to keep company with him who secretly slanders his neighbor. I refuse to favor him who has a haughty look and a proud and arrogant heart. My eyes [look with favor] upon the faithful of

the land. He who works deceit shall not dwell in my house; he who tells lies shall not continue in my presence. I declare all the wicked in the land are rooted up. Thank You, Lord, for helping me to stand for Your Word.
Psalm 101

162. Father, help us to bridle our negative passions, and change them to compassion. In our zeal to please You, Lord, let us take our cues from You, so as not to cause strife or misunderstanding. Keep us from making our own plans and asking You to bless them. Instead, we ask for Your plan so our path is already prepared, and our success [although not effortless] is assured.
Psalm 37:23; Romans 8:14;

163. I refuse to fret because of evildoers or be envious toward wrongdoers. They wither quickly like the grass and fade like the green herb. I trust in You Lord, I commit to do good, to dwell in this land and to cultivate faithfulness. I delight myself in You, Lord; and You are giving me the desires of my heart. I commit my ways to You, Lord, trusting in You, and You are bringing it to pass. You bring forth my righteousness as the light and my judgment as the noonday.[58]
Psalm 37:1-3, 6; John 14:10

164. I study God's Word, I am loving, and forgiving, lest Satan should take advantage of me. I refuse to be ignorant of his devices.[59]
2 Corinthians 2:11

165. Father, I declare that we, who You call Your own, are rebuilding the foundations of our nation; that we are raising up the foundations of many generations, repairing the breach and restoring the paths in which to dwell.[60] *Isaiah 58:12*

---

58   Rest in the Lord and wait patiently for Him; do not fret because of him who prospers in his way, because of the man who carries out wicked schemes. Cease from anger and forsake wrath; do not fret; it leads only to evildoing. Evildoers shall be cut off: but those that wait upon the Lord, shall inherit the earth.
Psalm 37:1-9
59   Since faith works by love, and we can't get our prayers answered unless we forgive, we will be target practice for Satan if we don't love and forgive.
Galatians 5:6; Matthew 6:14-15; 18:21-35; 2 Corinthians 2:1-11; Ephesians 4:27; James 5:8-9
60   We are restoring our nation to a habitable state for our Lord to dwell in. Therefore, we receive the Blessings we should have enjoyed for generations. *Isaiah 58:12*

Day XXIII
Promises, false reports, bribes, canceling assignments

166. You, Lord, have promised to hear us, to help us, to save us, and to use us to raise up and establish our land out of its present state of decline through The Blessing.[61] You have promised to preserve us. Thank You, Lord. Through God's blessing, we bring light and hope to our nation. We, the body of Christ, feed the poor, we help people find jobs, we teach people how to be self-sufficient, we bless the land, and it is fruitful and multiplies in every good thing.
Isaiah 49:8; Deuteronomy 15:4-8; Matthew 19:21;

167. Now is the day of salvation and the redeemed of the Lord say so!
Psalm 107:2; 2 Corinthians 6:1-2

168. Lord, You said You rebuke and chasten those You love; therefore, we choose to be zealous and quick to repent.
Revelation 3:19

169. Father, I declare that our leaders inquire of You as David did, are led by Your Spirit and succeed in doing Your perfect will so that the people are blessed.
1 Chronicles 14:8-17; Romans 8:14

170. I refuse to repeat or raise a false report or join with the wicked to be an unrighteous witness. I refuse to follow a crowd to do evil; nor will I bear witness at a trial so as to side with a multitude to pervert justice. Neither will I be partial to a poor man in his trial. If I see someone who hates me lying [helpless] under his load, I will refrain from leaving the man to cope with it alone, but will stop to help him. I refuse to pervert the justice due to our poor in his cause. I keep far from a false matter, I refuse to condemn to death the innocent and the righteous, and I refuse to justify and acquit the wicked. I refuse to take a bribe, for the bribe blinds those who have sight and perverts

---

61 Refers to The Blessing of *Genesis 1:28* to be fruitful and multiply to replenish the earth, subdue it and to have dominion.

the testimony and the cause of the righteous.
Exodus 23:1-8

"And now, O Lord, my God, Thou hast made thy servant ruler over the people. Give unto him an understanding heart that he may know how to go out and come in before this great people; that he may discern between good and bad. For who is able to judge this thy so great a people?' were the words of a royal Sovereign; and not less applicable to him who is invested with the Chief Magistracy of a nation, though he wear not a crown, nor robes of royalty."

Abigail Adams, on the occasion of her husband, John Adams' election as second president of the United States.

171. Today, I spend time in the Bible and in fellowship with God to strengthen myself and gain godly wisdom against those who would try to deceive me and take away my God-given rights and freedoms.
Proverbs 4:5-7; Exodus 20:1-17; Isaiah 61:1-3; Philemon 6; 2 Corinthians 9:8; 2 Timothy 6:17

172. We are free of quenching the Spirit or despising prophecies.

Day Twenty-Three

Instead we test all things, hold fast to what is good, and abstain from every form of evil.
1 Thessalonians 5:19-22

173. Devil, you are bound, and I cancel every assignment that you have against our nation and our Constitution in the name of Jesus Christ.[62]
Genesis 1:26; Matthew 18:18

Your Notes:

---

[62] And I will give unto thee the keys of the kingdom of heaven: and whatsoever thou shalt bind on earth shall be bound in heaven: and whatsoever thou shalt loose on earth shall be loosed in heaven. *Matthew 16:19*

Prayer For The Nation - *Mary Ervasti*

Your Notes:

Day XXIV
The U.S. Constitution; Unshakeable, judges,
laws established by the people[63]

174. Father, I thank You for Your hand in the creation of our U. S. Constitution. I declare it stands according to Your perfect Will. I declare it belongs to the people of the United States of America, and You designed it for our protection. I declare that our government is of the people, by the people, and for the people; and that we, as the people of God in the United States of America, declare that no weapon that is formed against us shall prosper; and every tongue that rises against us in judgment we do condemn. This is the heritage of the servants of the Lord, and our righteousness is of the Lord (see next page).
Isaiah 54:17; Job 22:28

175. I declare the Constitution of the United States of America is unshakeable because Your hand is upon our nation. It will stand against all who would try to misinterpret or rewrite it to an ungodly standard because the book of John says "Whatsoever ye shall ask in my name, that will I do, that the Father may be glorified in the Son."
Daniel 2: 20-21; John 14:13; 2 Timothy 1:7

176. I declare that we, the people, purge everything from our Constitution that has been called constitutional without any legal foundation.[64]
Psalm 119:117-119; Romans 13:7

177. Thank You God for our Declaration of Independence, our U.S. Constitution, and our Bill of Rights. Thank You that You have directed our founders, and that these foundational documents have

---
63 See **Appendix C** for additional background information.
64 "Whensoever the General Government assumes undelegated powers, its acts are unauthoritative, void, and of no force. The government created by this compact [*editor's note:* The U.S. Constitution] was not made the exclusive or final of the extent of the powers delegated to itself, since that would have made its discretion, and not the Constitution, the measure of its powers …"
Thomas Jefferson, 1798

Prayer For The Nation - Mary Ervasti

Give up money, give up fame, give up science, give the earth itself and all it contains rather than do an immoral act. And never suppose that in any possible situation, or under any circumstances, it is best for you to do a dishonorable thing, however slightly so it may appear to you. Whenever you are to do a thing, though it can never be known but to yourself, ask yourself how you would act were all the world looking at you, and act accordingly. Encourage all your virtuous dispositions, and exercise them whenever an opportunity arises, being assured that they will gain strength by exercise, as a limb of the body does, and that exercise will make them habitual. From the practice of the purest virtue, you may be assured you will derive the most sublime comforts in every moment of life, and in the moment of death.

Thomas Jefferson, Signer of the Declaration of Independence and Third President of the United States

Source: Thomas Jefferson, The Writings of Thomas Jefferson, Albert Bergh, editor (Washington, DC: Thomas Jefferson Memorial Assoc., 1903), Vol. 5, pp. 82-83, in a letter to his nephew Peter Carr on August 19, 1785.

helped us to govern our nation with liberty and justice established by the people.[65]
Exodus 18:21; 20:13; Deuteronomy 1:16-17; 19:17-19; Psalm 2:10-11; 119:45; Isaiah 61:1; Matthew 7:24; 2 Corinthians 3:17; Galatians 5:1, 13

178. Father, to reduce our debt we declare all government funding for any corrupt purpose is exposed and all unconstitutional spending is removed. We declare that the people who become unemployed because of these changes find jobs or have the insight, concepts, and ideas to create their own.
Psalm 94:7-13; Proverbs 1:7; Romans 13:8; Ephesians 6:10; Philippians 4:19

179. I declare all judges in this nation rule according to our Constitution, and with the wisdom of God interpret the spirit of the law. I declare they have a spirit of justice to judge and administer the law fairly, and have the strength to do so in a way that pleases God. Now therefore, I declare our leaders are teachable, and our judges hate bribes and covetousness. They judge all people equally and refuse to pervert justice. Instead, they serve the Lord with fear, and rejoice with trembling. They are wise and understanding and have mercy and compassion for everyone.
Psalm 1:10-12; Exodus 18:21; Deuteronomy 1:13,16,17; Isaiah 1:17; 28:6; James 1:5

180. We declare that all of our judges understand that their job is to enforce the law, promote justice, and uphold the Constitution. Furthermore, place clearly in the minds of all the Senators in the confirmation hearings the consequences of making choices based on their own desire to be re-elected, to be assigned to certain committees of power, or any other self-interest. Instead, I pray an anointing over the questions they ask the nominees that would clearly show the values, philosophies, and capabilities of those nominees by which they will make their decisions. Thank You, God for helping us to do this!

---

65 From the Declaration of Independence: "We hold these truths to be self-evident, that all men are created equal, that they are endowed by their Creator with certain unalienable rights that among these are life, liberty and the pursuit of happiness. - That to secure these rights, governments are instituted among men, deriving their just powers from the consent of the governed, - That whenever any form of government becomes destructive of these ends, it is the right of the people to alter or to abolish it, and to institute new government, laying its foundation on such principles and organizing its powers in such form, as to them shall seem most likely to effect their safety and happiness." (see Appendix A)
http://pftn.co/BTGow

Prayer For The Nation   -   Mary Ervasti

Isaiah 1:26; 5:18-24; Exodus 18:21; 23:3,6,8; 2 Samuel 23:3; Ezra 7:25; Deuteronomy 1:13; 16:18-19; 27:19; 25:1; Zechariah 7:9-10; Joshua 1:7-8

181. I declare that our President, every judge, senator, congressman, representative, governor, mayor, councilman and every government official yields to You, Father God, and does what You say.
Daniel 2:21

God shed His Grace on thee

n May 13, 1824, our first Chief Justice, John Jay, addressed the American Bible Society of which he was president:

"By conveying the Bible to people, we thereby enable them to learn that our gracious Creator has provided for us a Redeemer, that this Redeemer has made atonement 'for the sins of the whole world,' and thereby reconciling the Divine justice with the Divine mercy, has opened a way for our redemption and salvation; and that these inestimable benefits are the free gift and grace of God, not of our deserving, nor in our power to deserve."

In a world where people have so idolized self that they feel they deserve to be taken care of by someone else or another entity, whether it be corporations, government, etc., our first Supreme Court Chief Justice gave us a different perspective. He shows us that we don't deserve anything, even from God. However, God gives us Divine justice and Divine mercy anyway as a free gift. His grace makes a way that no man can make for himself, and He has promised to supply all of our needs.

Philippians 4:19

Day XXV
Hundred-fold return, liars destroyed, honor

182. I call for the hundred-fold return on all the prayers that our founders prayed over this nation. I declare our nation is holy, righteous, covered in God's glory and fulfills its purpose in the earth.
Job 22:8; Mark 4:8; Romans 4:17

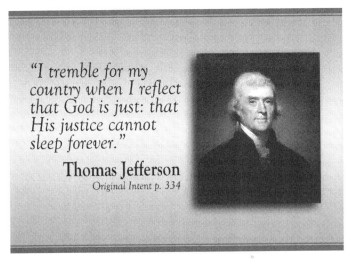

"I tremble for my country when I reflect that God is just: that His justice cannot sleep forever."
Thomas Jefferson
Original Intent p. 334

183. Thank you, Lord that You hate evil, and have promised to destroy all liars. Thank You that all those who think they are higher than You or know more than You will fall because they cannot stand in Your presence. However, I will worship You with deepest awe. Lead me in the right path, O Lord, or my enemies will conquer me. Make your way plain for me to follow.
Psalm 5:5-8; Proverbs 16:18; Romans 8:14

184. My enemies cannot speak a truthful word. Their deepest desire is to destroy others. Their talk is foul, like the stench from an open grave. Their tongues are filled with flattery. O God, declare them guilty. Let them be caught in their own traps. Drive them away because of their many sins, for they have rebelled against You. But I take refuge in You and rejoice, I sing joyful praises to You forever. Spread Your protection over us who love Your name so that we may be filled with joy. For You bless the godly, O Lord; You surround us

Prayer For The Nation - Mary Ervasti

with Your shield of love.
Psalm 5:9-12

185. Thank you, Lord, for all You have to say about government. I thank You that You have given us the ability to get wisdom and good judgment, and use it to appoint magistrates and judges to govern the people who know and obey Your laws.
Genesis 18:19; Ezra 7:25; Proverbs 4:5-7; 16:16; 19:8; James 1:5

186. We vote for and honor those who obey and enforce the law of this land, and we declare our leaders are just, ruling in the fear of God.
Exodus 18:21-22; 2 Samuel 23:3; Deuteronomy 1:13

187. You, Lord, are quick to testify against those who do not fear You – the sorcerers, adulterers, and perjurers, against those who defraud laborers of their wages, who oppress the widows and the fatherless, and deprive the foreigners among us of justice. You do not change. You have charged us with turning away from Your decrees and not keeping them. However, Your mercy endures forever, and You have promised that if we return to You, You will return to us. We ask Your forgiveness, thank You for Your mercy, and choose to return to Your ways.
Malachi 3:5-7; 1 Chronicles 16:34; James 5:4

188. Thank You God for honoring us who honor You. You said we who wait for You would not be ashamed that even the captives of the mighty shall be taken away, and the plunder of tyrants will be retrieved because You will contend with those that contend with us, and that You will save our children. We believe Your Word on this and stand for it.
Isaiah 49:23, 25; Mark 5:36; Luke 8:50

Your Notes:

Day XXVI
Love your neighbor, depart from sin, do God's commands

189. Father we have sat before You as Your people, and heard the words You say, but we have not done them. With our mouths we show much love, but our hearts are set on our [idolatrous greed for] gain. We ask for Your forgiveness, and Your grace to do what You say.
Ezekiel 33:31

190. I obey Your word that says, "Owe no one anything except to love one another, for he who loves another has fulfilled the law." For the commandments, "You shall not commit adultery," "You shall not murder," "You shall not steal," "You shall not bear false witness," "You shall not covet," are all summed up in this saying, namely, "You shall love your neighbor as yourself." Love does no harm to a neighbor; therefore, love is the fulfillment of God's law. I do this, knowing that now it is high time to awake out of sleep for now my salvation is nearer than when I first believed. The night is far spent; the day is at hand. Therefore, I cast off the works of darkness and put on the armor of light. I walk properly, as in the day, not in revelry and drunkenness, not in lewdness and lust, not in strife and envy. But I put on the Lord Jesus Christ, and make no provision for fulfilling the lusts of the flesh.
Joel 3:12; Romans 13:8-14

191. We overcome the world because we believe that Jesus is the Son of God. This is the victory that has overcome the world—our faith.
1 John 5:4, 5

192. Since love never fails, I love people the world over.
1 Corinthians 13:8

193. We love one another, even if that means tough love, and our faith works by love.
Galatians 5:6; 1 John 5:2

Prayer For The Nation - Mary Ervasti

194. We lay aside every sin, and depart from iniquity, honoring the name of Christ, fleeing youthful lusts, and following right living, faith, love, and peace, calling on the Lord out of a pure heart so that we are prepared for every good work and so that our right living exalts our nation.
Proverbs 14:34; Hebrews 12:1; 2 Timothy 2:19, 21-22; 1 Peter 3:12

195. I hear and diligently do God's commandments, love Him and serve Him with all my heart, refusing to serve the gods of money, self, power, or any other addiction, so that God prospers me.
Deuteronomy 11:13-14, 16; Romans 8:14

Your Notes:

Day XXVII
Justice, blessing, established and steady, judges

196. The wicked perish and vanish like smoke. For the Lord loves justice, and forsakes not his saints, who are preserved forever. The offspring of the wicked is cut off and the righteous inherit the land, and dwell there forever. The righteous speak of wisdom and justice. The law of his God is in his heart; none of his steps waver.
Psalm 37:20,28-31

197. I am blessed because I reverence and worship the Lord, and delight greatly in His commandments. My offspring are mighty upon the earth. The generation of the upright is blessed. Wealth and riches are in my house and my righteousness (in Christ) endures forever. Light arises in the darkness for me because I am upright, gracious, compassionate, and just. It is well with me because I deal generously and lend and conduct my affairs with justice. I refuse to be moved or shaken because I am in right standing with God. I am not afraid of evil tidings; my heart is firmly fixed trusting (leaning on and being confident) in the Lord. My heart is established and steady and I am free of fear while I wait to see my desire established upon my adversaries. I give freely to the poor and needy; my right standing with God endures forever. My power, strength, and dignity are honored. The wicked see it, are grieved, angered, and disappear in despair; their desires perishing and coming to nothing.
Psalm 112

198. I wash myself; make myself clean. I put away the evil of my doings from before God's eyes. I cease to do evil, and learn to do good. I seek justice, rebuke the oppressor, defend the fatherless, and plead for the widow. The Lord says, though our sins are like scarlet, they will be as white as snow. Though they are red like crimson, they shall be as wool. If I am willing and obedient, I will eat the good of the land, but if I refuse and rebel, I will be devoured by the sword for the mouth of the Lord has spoken.
Isaiah 1:16-20

199. Our cities were once full of justice, righteousness lodged in

them, but now murderers live in them. Our silver has become dross, our leaders are rebellious, and companions of thieves. People love bribes, and follow after rewards. They do not defend the fatherless, nor does the cause of the widow come before them. However, I agree with the Lord's answer to this and I declare that our leaders and judges humble themselves to be instructed. I declare they serve the Lord with fear, rejoice with trembling, and kiss the Son lest He be angry and they perish from God's way when His wrath is kindled but a little. We are blessed who put our trust in Him.
Exodus 18:21-22; Psalm 2:10-12; Daniel 2:21; Isaiah 1:21-26

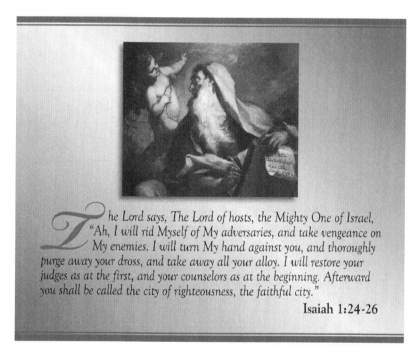

The Lord says, The Lord of hosts, the Mighty One of Israel, "Ah, I will rid Myself of My adversaries, and take vengeance on My enemies. I will turn My hand against you, and thoroughly purge away your dross, and take away all your alloy. I will restore your judges as at the first, and your counselors as at the beginning. Afterward you shall be called the city of righteousness, the faithful city."

Isaiah 1:24-26

200. We charge all of our judges that they judge righteously between a man and his brother or the stranger or sojourner who is with him.
Deuteronomy 1:16-17; 16:18-19; 25:1

201. We declare our judges are not partial in judgment, but they hear the small as well as the great. They are not afraid of the face of man, for they hear God's judgment and rule as He says and shows

Day Twenty-Seven

them.
Exodus Chapters 21-23; Deuteronomy 1:17

Your Notes:

Prayer For The Nation - Mary Ervasti

Your Notes:

Day XXVIII
Falsely accused and defended by God

202. We pray over our nation, especially for all who are falsely accused, as were our forefathers before the Revolutionary War.

Contend, Lord, with those who contend with our nation. Fight against those who fight against us. Come to our aid against those who pursue us. Say to us, "I am your salvation." We declare those who seek to destroy our lives are disgraced and put to shame, and those who plot our ruin are turned back in dismay. They are like chaff before the wind, with the angel of the Lord driving them away. Their path is dark and slippery, with the angel of the Lord pursuing them. Since they hid their net for us without cause and without cause dug a pit for us, their ruin overtakes them by surprise – the net they hid entangles them. They fall into the pit, to their ruin.

Then my soul will rejoice in the Lord and delight in his salvation. My whole being will exclaim, "Who is like you, Lord? You rescue the poor from those too strong for them, the poor and needy from those who rob them." Ruthless witnesses come forward, and they question us on things we know nothing about.

They repay us evil for good and leave us like one bereaved. Yet when they needed help, we sent our ships to help them. But when we stumbled, they gathered in glee; assailants gathered against us without our knowledge. They slandered us without ceasing. Like the ungodly they maliciously mocked and they gnashed their teeth at us.

How long, Lord, will you look on? Rescue us from their ravages, our precious lives from these lions. We will give you thanks in the great assembly; among the throngs we will praise you. Do not let those gloat over us who are our enemies without cause; do not let those who hate us without reason maliciously wink the eye.

Prayer For The Nation - Mary Ervasti

They do not speak peaceably, but devise false accusations against those who live quietly in the land. They sneer at us and say, "Aha! Aha! With our own eyes we have seen it." Lord, you have seen this; do not be silent. Do not be far from us, Lord. Awake, and rise to our defense! Contend for us. You are our God and Lord. Vindicate us in Your righteousness, oh Lord our God; do not let them gloat over us. Do not let them think, "Aha, just what we wanted!" or say, "We have swallowed them up."

May all who gloat over our distress be put to shame and confusion; may all who exalt themselves over us be clothed with shame and disgrace. May those who delight in our vindication shout for joy and gladness; may they always say, "The Lord be exalted, who delights in the prosperity of his servant." And my tongue shall speak of Thy righteousness and Thy praise all the day long.

I declare that You, Lord, are doing all that we ask in this prayer.[66]
Psalm 35; Job 22:28; John 15:7

Your Notes:

---

66 As the colonies saw that Boston was only the first target, and that the British would continue to attack, they began to unite, and called for a Congress of deputies from each province to be convened. This became America's first national Congress gathered in Philadelphia on September 5, 1774. On the first day of that Congress, they resolved to ask the Reverend Mr. Duche' to open the next session (on September 7, 1774) thus beginning the long tradition of opening Congress with prayer. That day, Reverend Duche' read the lesson for the 7th day of September which was the 35th Psalm. Let us pray this over our nation as they did. Original Intent, Wallbuilder Press, 2000, pp 92-94.

In addition, since our founders took the Word of God seriously, they believed they could count on God's promises to defend them. I suspect many were also tithers which meant the promises of Malachi would be theirs:

"Bring ye all the tithes into the storehouse, that there may be meat in mine house, and prove me now herewith, saith the Lord of hosts, if I will not open you the windows of heaven, and pour you out a blessing, that there shall not be room enough to receive it. And I will rebuke the devourer for your sakes, and he shall not destroy the fruits of your ground; neither shall your vine cast her fruit before the time in the field, saith the Lord of hosts." *Malachi 3:10-11*

Day Twenty-Eight

*A*fter the Boston Tea Party, Mercy Otis Warren reported that not only did the colonists pray, but they also began to organize relief for the Bostonians. The citizens of Pepperell, Massachusetts sent grain. Their leader, **William Prescott,** wrote to the Bostonians of the sympathy and support of those in Pepperell. He said, "Our forefathers passed the vast Atlantic, spent their blood and treasure that they might enjoy their liberties both civil and religious, and transmit them to their posterity...Now if we should give them up, can our children rise up and call us blessed?...Let us all be of one heart and stand fast in the liberty wherewith Christ has made us free; and may He of His infinite mercy grant us deliverance out of all our troubles."

Original Intent, Wallbuilder Press, 2000, pp 91-92

Galatians 5:1

Prayer For The Nation - *Mary Ervasti*

Your Notes:

Day XXIX
God will never leave us, repentance, protection

203. Even though we have done wicked things, You have promised never to leave us nor forsake us for Your name's sake. We repent and promise to turn away from that wickedness, asking Your forgiveness. We choose to follow and serve You with all our hearts.
Genesis 15:1; 26:24; 50:21; 1 Samuel 12:20-22, 24-25; Hebrews 13:5

204. I choose to turn away from all my offenses, so then sin will not be my downfall. You, Lord, will judge each of us according to our own ways. Help us to rid ourselves of all the offenses we have committed, and receive a new heart and a new spirit. You take no pleasure in the death of anyone, but the wages of sin is death. Help us to repent and live!
Ezekiel 18:30-32; Romans 6:23

205. We count it all joy when we are tested (for example being tested to think of others *vs.* ourselves), knowing that the trying of our faith to have the mind of Christ yields patience; and if we let patience finish her perfect work, we may be mature and complete.
James 1:2-4; 1 Corinthians 2:16

206. We declare that we dwell in the Secret Place of the Most High, and abide under the shadow of You Almighty Father. You are our refuge and our fortress, our God. On You, we lean and rely. In You we confidently trust. You deliver us from the snare of the fowler (the devil fowling things up for us), and the deadly pestilence. You cover us with Your pinions, and under Your wings, we trust and have refuge. Your truth and faithfulness are our shield and buckler. We are free of the fear of the terror of the night, and of the evil plots and slanders of the wicked that fly by day. We love. Therefore, fear has no place. A thousand fearful thoughts and arrows from the devil may fall at our sides, and 10,000 fall at our right hand, but none takes root in us, or even comes near us. We see the reward of the wicked from the Secret Place. No evil befalls us, nor any calamity or plague comes near our homes. For You, Father, have given Your angels charge over us to accompany, defend, and preserve our family in all our ways of

Prayer For The Nation - Mary Ervasti

obedience and service. Because we have, and continue to make, You, Lord, our refuge and our dwelling place, these angels bear us up on their hands, lest we dash our feet against a stone. We tread upon the lion and adder, and trample the young lion and serpent under our feet. Because we set our love upon You, You deliver us and set us on high because we know and understand Your name, and have personal knowledge of Your mercy, love, and kindness, because we trust and rely on You, knowing You will never forsake us, no, NEVER! We call upon You and you answer us when we ask questions and make requests of you. You are with us in trouble. You deliver us and honor us. With long life, You satisfy us and show us Your salvation.
Psalm 91

207. Lord, You warn that those who rely on their sword, do detestable things, and defile their neighbor's wife should not possess the land. For those who are evil will be destroyed, but those who hope in the Lord will inherit the land. We place our hope in You, Lord, for ourselves and the salvation of those doing evil.
Psalm 37:9; Ezekiel 33:26

208. Thank You, Lord, that You have promised that the arm of the wicked shall be broken, but that You uphold the righteous; that You know the days of the upright, their inheritance shall be forever, they shall not be ashamed in the evil time, and in the days of famine they shall be satisfied. I take these promises as my own, and stand for them.
Psalm 37:17-19; Ephesians 6:10-18

209. I promise to return to You, Lord, to stop stealing from You, and to give You my tithes so You can use them to prosper me, my house, the body of Christ, and my nation. You have given me the power to get wealth in order to establish Your covenant of Blessing to be fruitful, multiply, and replenish the earth. I declare the laws of *Progresssive Increase* are the result of my tithing causing me to have an abundantly increasing, continuously flowing supply of everything good. Therefore, I choose to give more and be multiplied, again and again.[67]

---

67   Progressive Increase would be:
Stage 1 -- it shall be given unto you; good measure

Day Twenty-Nine

Genesis 1:27-28; 26:12; Proverbs 19:17; Malachi 3:8-10; Deuteronomy 8:18; Mark 4:20, 30; Luke 6:38

"He who stands for nothing will fall for anything."

Spoken by the great patriot **Alexander Hamilton** in the heat of battle during the American Revolution. Often, society hasn't stood for what's right because we think it's impossible to achieve. What we're really saying is that we don't believe God when He says all things are possible with Him, and we don't believe it because **we haven't developed our faith** to hear from God. However, that just takes practice like learning anything else. Faith comes by hearing the Word of God.

Matthew 19:26; Mark 10:27; Luke 1:37; Romans 8:14

Your Notes:

Stage 2 -- it shall be given unto you pressed down
Stage 3 -- it shall be given unto you shaken together
Stage 4 -- it shall be given unto you running over, shall men give into your bosom Luke 6:38
To see more about Progressive Increase, go to:
http://bit.ly/190actf

Prayer For The Nation - Mary Ervasti

Your Notes:

Day XXX
Reverence, hypocrisy, envy

210. We believe and declare that because we reverence You, Lord, serve, obey, and refuse to rebel against Your commandments, that our leaders follow You. We praise You and thank You, Lord, that even though we have sinned, You forgive us when we ask for forgiveness.
1 Samuel 12:14-15; 20,22; Hebrews 13:15

211. The willful are destroyed together, and the end of the wicked is that they are cut off. But the salvation of the righteous is of the Lord, and He is our strength in the time of trouble. The Lord is helping us, delivering us from the wicked, and saving us, because we trust in Him.
Psalm 37:38-40

212. We lay aside all malice, guile, hypocrisy, envy, and all evil speaking, desiring the sincere milk of the Word, that we may grow and be built up in our spiritual house, so that we grow into a full experience of salvation, becoming a holy priesthood acceptable to God by Jesus Christ, and unashamed of it.
1 Peter 2:1-2, 5-6

213. I choose to act out of a pure heart, or a good conscience and genuine faith. I examine myself daily so that I am not speaking vain words, desiring to hear myself talk, and thinking I can teach others when I have little understanding.
1 Timothy 1:5-7; Ephesians 5:6

214. We are fortunate and blessed because we revere and worship God and delight in His commandments. Because of this, wealth and riches are in our houses and our righteousness endures forever.
Psalm 112:1, 3

Prayer For The Nation - Mary Ervasti

Your Notes:

Day XXXI
Arrogance, political correctness, continuous supply

215. Thank You, Lord, that you never leave me comfortless, but You come to me.
John 14:18

216. I keep God's Word, and the love of God is perfected in me. I love my brothers and sisters with the love of God that is in me, because He dwells in me.
1 John 2:5; 4:12

217. Pride goes before destruction and a haughty spirit before a fall. Therefore, we refuse to be high-minded, self-righteous, or arrogant.
Proverbs 16:18

218. I refuse to fret because of evildoers for they will soon be cut down like the grass. I refuse to fret because it tends only to evildoing. Evildoers are being cut off, but those who wait on the Lord inherit the earth.
Psalm 37:2,8-9

219. Father, I refuse political correctness in favor of the truth. I refuse to be muzzled, but instead, hear from God and speak words to the weary in due season. I refuse to fear mere men, for God has not given us the spirit of fear, but of power, and of love, and of a sound mind. I trust God and the appropriate words are given to me.[68] I'm

---

68 **Crushing Fear**
Some years ago, I had a very strong fear and I had counseled with a Christian therapist about it. My husband, Dick, was very supportive and had gone to some of the counseling sessions with me. However, my counselor told me that I would have to confront the people concerned and it would be best if I did it without Dick. I needed to stand alone.

Over the course of that summer, every day I recited the scripture, "I am free of the spirit of fear. Instead, I have the spirit of power, love and a sound mind." That autumn, the day came when I needed to confront those involved. I prayed for an anointing to remove burdens and destroy yokes of bondage (*ie*, the bondage of fear). As I confronted my fears, stood alone, and said my piece, the anointing was on me and the power of that scripture repeated day after day over that summer was powerful in me.

I was able to confront that situation with love, not anger. The love that grew between me

strong in the Lord and in the power of His might.
Isaiah 50:4; Matthew 10:19; Mark 7:13; Ephesians 6:10; Romans 8:14; 2 Timothy 1:7

220. I choose to love my enemies, bless them that curse me, do good to them that hate me, and pray for those who despitefully use and persecute me, as Jesus commanded.
Matthew 5:44

221. We have an abundantly increasing, continuously flowing supply of everything we need because God supplies all of our needs according to His riches in glory by Christ Jesus, and because He came that we might have life more abundantly!
John 10:10; Philippians 4:19

222. Thank You, Lord, that Your Word does not return to You void, but it accomplishes that which You please, and it prospers in the thing where You send it. You sent Your Word and healed them, and delivered them from their destructions. We declare that as we return Your Word to You in these prayers, that You will deliver us from our destructions and heal our nation because You are no respecter of persons.
Psalm 107:20; Isaiah 55:11; Acts 10:34

223. Thank You, God, that you are able to make all grace abound toward us; that we always, having all sufficiency in all things, may abound to every good work.
2 Corinthians 9:8

224. Lord we choose to hear Your Word in the Bible. We choose to say it out loud to ourselves over and over so that we program Your truth into us. We choose to level the playing field of input into our lives day after day by hearing the truth of Your Word spoken out loud to ourselves so that we can build ourselves up in faith. We declare that as we create faith in ourselves this way, when the time

---

and the people involved from that point was remarkable. The relationship shifted from one of abuse to one of respect, which I enjoy to this day.

Day Thirty-One

comes that we need to stand for You, and for what's right, we will have the faith to do it. Your Word and Your promises are The Truth. Even though there may be differing facts, Your Word is still the highest Word. We choose to get understanding on this Truth.
Proverbs 4:7; Matthew 19:26; Mark 10:27; Luke 1:37

"IN GOD WE TRUST"

*Repeat these prayers every month
beginning with Day I.*

Your Notes:

Visit our website at:

PrayerForTheNation.com

It's in your hands.

Become a member of our PFTN Prayer Team

- Submit prayer requests & praise reports
- Pray for specific areas based on zip & postal codes with PFTN PrayerZIP®
- Get books, bible studies, downloads and Christian travel packages - ALL often for free or at deep discounts when you become a subscriber. *TRIAL OFFER - $1 for 12 weeks!*

Sign up today at:
www.PFTN.co/pzip

Prayer For The Nation   -   Mary Ervasti

Appendix A - The U.S. Declaration of Independence

Appendix A

The United States Declaration of Independence

IN CONGRESS, JULY 4, 1776

The unanimous Declaration of the thirteen United States of America

When in the Course of human events it becomes necessary for one people to dissolve the political bands which have connected them with another and to assume among the powers of the earth, the separate and equal station to which the Laws of Nature and of Nature's God[69] entitle them, a decent respect to the opinions of mankind requires that they should declare the causes which impel them to the separation.

We hold these truths to be self-evident, that all men are created equal, that they are endowed by their Creator with certain unalienable Rights, that among these are Life, Liberty, and the pursuit of Happiness[70] — That to secure these rights, Governments are instituted among Men, deriving their just powers from the consent of the governed, — That whenever any Form of Government becomes destructive of these ends, it is the Right of the People to alter or to abolish it, and to institute new Government, laying its foundation on such principles and organizing its powers in such form, as to them shall seem most likely to effect their Safety and Happiness.[71] Prudence, indeed, will dictate that Governments long established should not be changed for light and transient causes; and accordingly all experience hath shewn that mankind are more disposed to suffer, while evils are sufferable than to right themselves by abolishing the forms to which they are accustomed.[72] But when a long train of abuses and

---

69 As created beings, we are subject to our Maker's (*ie*, God's) will, called the Laws of Nature. Pg 166, *The Founder's Bible*, paraphrase by William Blackstone.
70 *Exodus 20:13; Psalm 119:45; Isaiah 61:1; Romans 8:21; 2 Corinthians 3:17; Galatians 5:1, 13; James 1:25; 2 Corinthians 9:8*
71 *Leviticus 25:18-19; Deuteronomy 33:26-29*
72 *Exodux 20:1-17; James 1:1-8*

usurpations, pursuing invariably the same Object evinces a design to reduce them under absolute Despotism, it is their right, it is their duty, to throw off such Government, and to provide new Guards for their future security. — Such has been the patient sufferance of these Colonies; and such is now the necessity which constrains them to alter their former Systems of Government. The history of the present King of Great Britain is a history of repeated injuries and usurpations, all having in direct object the establishment of an absolute Tyranny over these States. To prove this, let Facts be submitted to a candid world.

He has refused his Assent to Laws, the most wholesome and necessary for the public good.

He has forbidden his Governors to pass Laws of immediate and pressing importance, unless suspended in their operation till his Assent should be obtained; and when so suspended, he has utterly neglected to attend to them.[73]

He has refused to pass other Laws for the accommodation of large districts of people, unless those people would relinquish the right of Representation in the Legislature, a right inestimable to them and formidable to tyrants only.[74]

He has called together legislative bodies at places unusual, uncomfortable, and distant from the depository of their Public Records, for the sole purpose of fatiguing them into compliance with his measures.[75]

He has dissolved Representative Houses repeatedly, for opposing with manly firmness his invasions on the rights of the people.

He has refused for a long time, after such dissolutions, to cause others to be elected, whereby the Legislative Powers, incapable of Annihilation, have returned to the People at large for their exercise; the State remaining in the mean time exposed to all the dangers of invasion from without, and convulsions within.

He has endeavoured to prevent the population of these States; for that purpose obstructing the Laws for Naturalization of Foreigners; refusing to pass others to encourage their migrations hither, and rais-

---

73 *Deuteronomy 1:13; 2 Chronicles 1:8-12*
74 *Exodus 18:21; Daniel 2:21*
75 *Deuteronomy 16:19; Psalm 10:1-4*

Appendix A - The U.S. Declaration of Independence

ing the conditions of new Appropriations of Lands.[76]

He has obstructed the Administration of Justice by refusing his Assent to Laws for establishing Judiciary Powers.

He has made Judges dependent on his Will alone for the tenure of their offices, and the amount and payment of their salaries.

He has erected a multitude of New Offices, and sent hither swarms of Officers to harass our people and eat out their substance.

He has kept among us, in times of peace, Standing Armies without the Consent of our legislatures.

He has affected to render the Military independent of and superior to the Civil Power.

He has combined with others to subject us to a jurisdiction foreign to our constitution, and unacknowledged by our laws; giving his Assent to their Acts of pretended Legislation:

For quartering large bodies of armed troops among us:

For protecting them, by a mock Trial from punishment for any Murders which they should commit on the Inhabitants of these States:[77]

For cutting off our Trade with all parts of the world:

For imposing Taxes on us without our Consent:

For depriving us in many cases, of the benefit of Trial by Jury:

For transporting us beyond Seas to be tried for pretended offences:

For abolishing the free System of English Laws in a neighbouring Province, establishing therein an Arbitrary government, and enlarging its Boundaries so as to render it at once an example and fit instrument for introducing the same absolute rule into these Colonies:

For taking away our Charters, abolishing our most valuable Laws and altering fundamentally the Forms of our Governments:

For suspending our own Legislatures, and declaring themselves invested with power to legislate for us in all cases whatsoever.

He has abdicated Government here, by declaring us out of his

---

76   *2 Samuel 23:3*
77   *John 8:44*

Prayer For The Nation - Mary Ervasti

Protection and waging War against us.

He has plundered our seas, ravaged our coasts, burnt our towns, and destroyed the lives of our people.[78]

He is at this time transporting large Armies of foreign Mercenaries to complete the works of death, desolation, and tyranny, already begun with circumstances of Cruelty & Perfidy scarcely paralleled in the most barbarous ages, and totally unworthy the Head of a civilized nation.

He has constrained our fellow Citizens taken Captive on the high Seas to bear Arms against their Country, to become the executioners of their friends and Brethren, or to fall themselves by their Hands.

He has excited domestic insurrections amongst us, and has endeavoured to bring on the inhabitants of our frontiers, the merciless Indian Savages whose known rule of warfare is an undistinguished destruction of all ages, sexes and conditions.

In every stage of these Oppressions We have Petitioned for Redress in the most humble terms: Our repeated Petitions have been answered only by repeated injury. A Prince, whose character is thus marked by every act which may define a Tyrant, is unfit to be the ruler of a free people.[79]

Nor have we been wanting in attentions to our British brethren. We have warned them from time to time of attempts by their legislature to extend an unwarrantable jurisdiction over us. We have reminded them of the circumstances of our emigration and settlement here. We have appealed to their native justice and magnanimity, and we have conjured them by the ties of our common kindred to disavow these usurpations, which would inevitably interrupt our connections and correspondence. They too have been deaf to the voice of justice and of consanguinity. We must, therefore, acquiesce in the necessity, which denounces our Separation, and hold them, as we hold the rest of mankind, Enemies in War, in Peace Friends.

We, therefore, the Representatives of the united States of America, in General Congress, Assembled, appealing to the Supreme Judge of the world for the rectitude of our intentions, do, in the Name, and by Authority of the good People of these Colonies, solemnly publish

---
78   *Exodus 20:13,15,16*
79   *1 Samuel 2:30*

Appendix A - The U.S. Declaration of Independence

and declare, That these united Colonies are, and of Right ought to be Free and Independent States, that they are Absolved from all Allegiance to the British Crown, and that all political connection between them and the State of Great Britain, is and ought to be totally dissolved; and that as Free and Independent States, they have full Power to levy War, conclude Peace, contract Alliances, establish Commerce, and to do all other Acts and Things which Independent States may of right do. And for the support of this Declaration, with a firm reliance on the protection of Divine Providence, we mutually pledge to each other our Lives, our Fortunes, and our sacred Honor.[80]
(Ed. note: See sidebar graphic on pg. 129)

Your Notes:

---

80 *2 Corinthians 10:4-5; Psalm 40:4*

Prayer For The Nation - Mary Ervasti

Regarding the Declaration of Independence, Abraham Lincoln said:

These communities, by their representatives in old Independence Hall, said to the whole world of men: "We hold these truths to be self-evident: that all men are created equal; that they are endowed by their Creator with certain inalienable rights; that among these are life, liberty, and the pursuit of happiness."....They erected a beacon to guide their children, and their children's children, and the countless myriads who should inhabit the earth in other ages....[T]hey established these great self-evident truths that...their posterity might look up again to the Declaration of Independence and take courage to renew that battle which their fathers began, so that truth and justice and mercy and all the humane and Christian virtues might not be extinguished from the land...Now, my countrymen, if you have been taught doctrines conflicting with the great landmarks of the Declaration of Independence...let me entreat you to come back...[C]ome back to the truths that are in the Declaration of Independence.

excerpt from Original Intent, Wallbuilder Press, 2000, p. 250

Appendix B

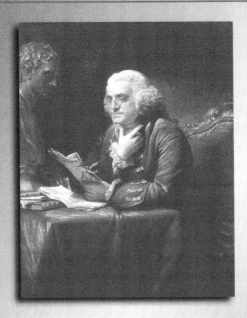

When the Constitutional Convention finally concluded, some delegates opposed the final document. However, perhaps Benjamin Franklin summed up the sense of the thirty-nine who signed it when he declared:

"I beg I may not be understood to infer that our general Convention was divinely inspired when it formed the new federal Constitution...yet I must own I have so much faith in the general government of the world by Providence that I can hardly conceive a transaction of such momentous importance to the welfare of millions now existing (and to exist in the posterity of a great nation) should be suffered to pass without being in some degree influenced, guided and governed by that omnipotent, omnipresent, and beneficient Ruler in whom all inferior spirits live, and move and have their being."

Acts 17:28
excerpt from *Original Intent* p. 112

Prayer For The Nation - *Mary Ervasti*

Your Notes:

Appendix B - The U.S. Constitution

Appendix B (con't)

THE UNITED STATES CONSTITUTION

We the People of the United States, in Order to form a more perfect Union, establish Justice, insure domestic Tranquility, provide for the common defence, promote the general Welfare, and secure the Blessings of Liberty to ourselves and our Posterity, do ordain and establish this Constitution for the United States of America.

Article. I.

Section 1.

All legislative Powers herein granted shall be vested in a Congress of the United States, which shall consist of a Senate and House of Representatives.

Section 2.

Clause 1: The House of Representatives shall be composed of Members chosen every second year by the People of the several States, and the Electors in each State shall have the Qualifications requisite for Electors of the most numerous Branch of the State Legislature.

Clause 2: No Person shall be a Representative who shall not have attained to the Age of twenty five years, and been seven years a Citizen of the United States, and who shall not, when elected, be an Inhabitant of that State in which he shall be chosen.

Clause 3: Representatives and direct Taxes shall be apportioned among the several States which may be included within this Union, according to their respective Numbers, which shall be determined by adding to the whole Number of free Persons, including those bound to Service for a Term of years, and excluding Indians not taxed, three fifths of all other Persons. The actual Enumeration shall be made within three years after the first Meeting of the Congress of the United States, and within every subsequent Term of ten years, in such Manner as they shall by Law direct. The Number of Representatives shall not exceed one for every thirty Thousand, but each State shall have at Least one Representative; and until such enumeration shall be made, the State of New Hampshire shall be entitled to choose three, Massachoosetts eight, Rhode-Island and Providence Plantations one, Connecticut five, New-York six, New Jersey four, Pennsylvania eight, Delaware one, Maryland six, Virginia ten, North Carolina five, South Carolina five, and Georgia three.

Clause 4: When vacancies happen in the Representation from any State, the Executive Authority thereof shall issue Writs of Election to fill such Vacancies.

Clause 5: The House of Representatives shall choose their Speaker and other Officers; and shall have the sole Power of Impeachment.

Section. 3.

Clause 1: The Senate of the United States shall be composed of two Senators from each State, chosen by the Legislature thereof, for six years; and each Senator shall have one Vote.

Clause 2: Immediately after they shall be assembled in Consequence of the first Election, they shall be divided as equally as may be into three Classes. The Seats of the Senators of the first Class shall be vacated at the Expiration of the second year, of the second Class at the Expiration of the fourth year, and of the third Class at the Expiration of the sixth year, so that one third may be chosen every second year; and if Vacancies happen by Resignation, or otherwise, during the Recess of the Legislature of any State, the Executive thereof may make temporary Appointments until the next Meeting of the Legislature, which shall then fill such Vacancies.

Clause 3: No Person shall be a Senator who shall not have attained to the Age of thirty years, and been nine years a Citizen of the United States, and who shall not, when elected, be an Inhabitant of that State for which he shall be chosen.

Clause 4: The Vice President of the United States shall be President of the Senate, but shall have no Vote, unless they be equally divided.

Clause 5: The Senate shall choose their other Officers, and also a President pro tempore, in the Absence of the Vice President, or when he shall exercise the Office of President of the United States.

Clause 6: The Senate shall have the sole Power to try all Impeachments. When sitting for that Purpose, they shall be on Oath or Affirmation. When the President of the United States is tried, the Chief Justice shall preside: And no Person shall be convicted without the Concurrence of two thirds of the Members present.

Clause 7: Judgment in Cases of Impeachment shall not extend further than to removal from Office, and disqualification to hold and enjoy any Office of honor, Trust or Profit under the United States: but the Party convicted shall nevertheless be liable and subject to Indictment, Trial, Judgment and Punishment, according to Law.

Section. 4.

Clause 1: The Times, Places and Manner of holding Elections for Senators and Representatives, shall be prescribed in each State by the Legislature thereof; but the Congress may at any time by Law make or alter such Regulations, except as to the Places of choosing Senators.

Clause 2: The Congress shall assemble at least once in every year, and such Meeting shall be on the first Monday in December, unless they shall by Law appoint a different Day.

Section. 5.

Clause 1: Each House shall be the Judge of the Elections, Returns and Qualifications of its own Members, and a Majority of each shall constitute a Quorum to do Business; but a smaller Number may adjourn from day to day, and may be authorized to compel the Attendance of absent Members, in such Manner, and under such Penalties as each House may provide.

Clause 2: Each House may determine the Rules of its Proceedings, punish its Members for disorderly Behaviour, and, with the Concurrence of two thirds, expel a Member.

Clause 3: Each House shall keep a Journal of its Proceedings, and from time to time publish the same, excepting such Parts as may in their Judgment require Secrecy; and the yeas and nays of the Members of either House on any question shall, at the Desire of one fifth of those Present, be entered on the Journal.

Clause 4: Neither House, during the Session of Congress, shall, without the Consent of the other, adjourn for more than three days, nor to any other Place than that in which the two Houses shall be sitting.

Section. 6.

Clause 1: The Senators and Representatives shall receive a Compensation for their Services, to be ascertained by Law, and paid out of the Treasury of the United States. They shall in all Cases, except Treason, Felony and Breach of the Peace, be privileged from Arrest during their Attendance at the Session of their respective Houses, and in going to and returning from the same; and for any Speech or Debate in either House, they shall not be questioned in any other Place.

Clause 2: No Senator or Representative shall, during the Time for which he was elected, be appointed to any civil Office under the Authority of the United States, which shall have been created, or the Emoluments whereof shall have been increased during such time; and no Person holding any Office under the United States, shall be a Member of either House during his Continuance in Office.

Section. 7.

Clause 1: All Bills for raising Revenue shall originate in the House of Representatives; but the Senate may propose or concur with Amendments as on other Bills.

Clause 2: Every Bill which shall have passed the House of Representatives and the Senate, shall, before it become a Law, be presented to the President of the United States; If he approve he shall sign it, but if not he shall return it, with his Objections to that House in which it shall have originated, who shall enter the Objections at large on their Journal, and proceed to reconsider it. If after such Reconsideration two thirds of that House shall agree to pass the Bill, it shall be sent, together with the Objections, to the other House, by which it shall likewise be reconsidered, and if approved by two thirds of that House, it shall become a Law. But in all such Cases the Votes of both Houses shall be determined by yeas and nays, and the Names of the Persons voting for and against the Bill shall be entered on the Journal of each House respectively. If any Bill shall not be returned by the President within ten Days (Sundays excepted) after it shall have been presented to him, the Same shall be a Law, in like Manner as if he had signed it, unless the Congress by their Adjournment prevent its Return, in which Case it shall not be a Law.

Clause 3: Every Order, Resolution, or Vote to which the Concurrence of the Senate and House of Representatives may be necessary (except on a question of Adjournment) shall be presented to the President of the United States; and before the Same shall take Effect, shall be approved by him, or being disapproved by him, shall be repassed by two thirds of the Senate and House of Representatives, according to the Rules and Limitations prescribed in the Case of a Bill.

Section. 8. [81]

Clause 1: The Congress shall have Power To lay and collect Taxes, Duties, Imposts and Excises, to pay the Debts and provide for the common Defence and general Welfare of the United States; but all Duties, Imposts and Excises shall be uniform throughout the United States;

Clause 2: To borrow Money on the credit of the United States;

Clause 3: To regulate Commerce with foreign Nations, and among the several States, and with the Indian Tribes;

Clause 4: To establish an uniform Rule of Naturalization, and uniform Laws on the subject of Bankruptcies throughout the United States;

Clause 5: To coin Money, regulate the Value thereof, and of foreign Coin, and fix the Standard of Weights and Measures;

Clause 6: To provide for the Punishment of counterfeiting the

---

81 "The American Republic will endure until the day Congress discovers that it can bribe the public with the public's money." **Alexis de Tocqueville**

Securities and current Coin of the United States;

Clause 7: To establish Post Offices and post Roads;

Clause 8: To promote the Progress of Science and useful Arts, by securing for limited Times to Authors and Inventors the exclusive Right to their respective Writings and Discoveries;

Clause 9: To constitute Tribunals inferior to the Supreme Court;

Clause 10: To define and punish Piracies and Felonies committed on the high Seas, and Offences against the Law of Nations;

Clause 11: To declare War, grant Letters of Marque and Reprisal, and make Rules concerning Captures on Land and Water;

Clause 12: To raise and support Armies, but no Appropriation of Money to that Use shall be for a longer Term than two years;

Clause 13: To provide and maintain a Navy;

Clause 14: To make Rules for the Government and Regulation of the land and naval Forces;

Clause 15: To provide for calling forth the Militia to execute the Laws of the Union, suppress Insurrections and repel Invasions;

Clause 16: To provide for organizing, arming, and disciplining, the Militia, and for governing such Part of them as may be employed in the Service of the United States, reserving to the States respectively, the Appointment of the Officers, and the Authority of training the Militia according to the discipline prescribed by Congress;

Clause 17: To exercise exclusive Legislation in all Cases whatsoever, over such District (not exceeding ten Miles square) as may, by Cession of particular States, and the Acceptance of Congress, become the Seat of the Government of the United States, and to exercise like Authority over all Places purchased by the Consent of the Legislature of the State in which the Same shall be, for the Erection of Forts, Magazines, Arsenals, dock-Yards, and other needful Buildings;--And

Clause 18: To make all Laws which shall be necessary and proper for carrying into Execution the foregoing Powers, and all other Powers vested by this Constitution in the Government of the United States, or in any Department or Officer thereof.

Appendix B - The U.S. Constitution

Section. 9.

Clause 1: The Migration or Importation of such Persons as any of the States now existing shall think proper to admit, shall not be prohibited by the Congress prior to the year one thousand eight hundred and eight, but a Tax or duty may be imposed on such Importation, not exceeding ten dollars for each Person.

Clause 2: The Privilege of the Writ of Habeas Corpus shall not be suspended, unless when in Cases of Rebellion or Invasion the public Safety may require it.

Clause 3: No Bill of Attainder or ex post facto Law shall be passed.

Clause 4: No Capitation, or other direct, Tax shall be laid, unless in Proportion to the Census or Enumeration herein before directed to be taken.

Clause 5: No Tax or Duty shall be laid on Articles exported from any State.

Clause 6: No Preference shall be given by any Regulation of Commerce or Revenue to the Ports of one State over those of another: nor shall Vessels bound to, or from, one State, be obliged to enter, clear, or pay Duties in another.

Clause 7: No Money shall be drawn from the Treasury, but in Consequence of Appropriations made by Law; and a regular Statement and Account of the Receipts and Expenditures of all public Money shall be published from time to time.

Clause 8: No Title of Nobility shall be granted by the United States: And no Person holding any Office of Profit or Trust under them, shall, without the Consent of the Congress, accept of any present, Emolument, Office, or Title, of any kind whatever, from any King, Prince, or foreign State.

Section. 10.

Clause 1: No State shall enter into any Treaty, Alliance, or Confederation; grant Letters of Marque and Reprisal; coin Money; emit Bills of Credit; make any Thing but gold and silver Coin a Tender in Payment of Debts; pass any Bill of Attainder, ex post facto Law, or Law impairing the Obligation of Contracts, or grant any Title of Nobility.

Clause 2: No State shall, without the Consent of the Congress, lay any Imposts or Duties on Imports or Exports, except what may be absolutely necessary for executing it's inspection Laws: and the net Produce of all Duties and Imposts, laid by any State on Imports or Exports, shall be for the Use of the Treasury of the United States; and all such Laws shall be subject to the Revision and Controul of the Congress.

Clause 3: No State shall, without the Consent of Congress, lay any Duty of Tonnage, keep Troops, or Ships of War in time of Peace, enter into any Agreement or Compact with another State, or with a foreign Power, or engage in War, unless actually invaded, or in such imminent Danger as will not admit of delay.

Article. II.

Section. 1.

Clause 1: The executive Power shall be vested in a President of the United States of America. He shall hold his Office during the Term of four years, and, together with the Vice President, chosen for the same Term, be elected, as follows

Clause 2: Each State shall appoint, in such Manner as the Legislature thereof may direct, a Number of Electors, equal to the whole Number of Senators and Representatives to which the State may be entitled in the Congress: but no Senator or Representative, or Person holding an Office of Trust or Profit under the United States, shall be appointed an Elector.

Clause 3: The Electors shall meet in their respective States, and vote by Ballot for two Persons, of whom one at least shall not be an Inhabitant of the same State with themselves. And they shall make a List of all the Persons voted for, and of the Number of Votes for each; which List they shall sign and certify, and transmit sealed to the Seat of the Government of the United States, directed to the President of the Senate. The President of the Senate shall, in the Presence of the

Appendix B - The U.S. Constitution

Senate and House of Representatives, open all the Certificates, and the Votes shall then be counted. The Person having the greatest Number of Votes shall be the President, if such Number be a Majority of the whole Number of Electors appointed; and if there be more than one who have such Majority, and have an equal Number of Votes, then the House of Representatives shall immediately choose by Ballot one of them for President; and if no Person have a Majority, then from the five highest on the List the said House shall in like Manner choose the President. But in choosing the President, the Votes shall be taken by States, the Representation from each State having one Vote; a quorum for this Purpose shall consist of a Member or Members from two thirds of the States, and a Majority of all the States shall be necessary to a Choice. In every Case, after the Choice of the President, the Person having the greatest Number of Votes of the Electors shall be the Vice President. But if there should remain two or more who have equal Votes, the Senate shall choose from them by Ballot the Vice President. (The preceding section has been superseded by the Twelfth Amendment.)

Clause 4: The Congress may determine the Time of choosing the Electors, and the Day on which they shall give their Votes; which Day shall be the same throughout the United States.

Clause 5: No Person except a natural born Citizen, or a Citizen of the United States, at the time of the Adoption of this Constitution, shall be eligible to the Office of President; neither shall any Person be eligible to that Office who shall not have attained to the Age of thirty five years, and been fourteen years a Resident within the United States.

Clause 6: In Case of the Removal of the President from Office, or of his Death, Resignation, or Inability to discharge the Powers and Duties of the said Office, the Same shall devolve on the Vice President, and the Congress may by Law provide for the Case of Removal, Death, Resignation or Inability, both of the President and Vice President, declaring what Officer shall then act as President, and such Officer shall act accordingly, until the Disability be removed, or a President shall be elected.

Clause 7: The President shall, at stated Times, receive for his Services, a Compensation, which shall neither be increased nor diminished during the Period for which he shall have been elected, and he shall not receive within that Period any other Emolument from the United States, or any of them.

Clause 8: Before he enter on the Execution of his Office, he shall take the following Oath or Affirmation:--"I do solemnly swear (or affirm) that I will faithfully execute the Office of President of the United States, and will to the best of my Ability, preserve, protect and defend the Constitution of the United States."

Section. 2.

Clause 1: The President shall be Commander in Chief of the Army and Navy of the United States, and of the Militia of the several States, when called into the actual Service of the United States; he may require the Opinion, in writing, of the principal Officer in each of the executive Departments, upon any Subject relating to the Duties of their respective Offices, and he shall have Power to grant Reprieves and Pardons for Offences against the United States, except in Cases of Impeachment.

Clause 2: He shall have Power, by and with the Advice and Consent of the Senate, to make Treaties, provided two thirds of the Senators present concur; and he shall nominate, and by and with the Advice and Consent of the Senate, shall appoint Ambassadors, other public Ministers and Consuls, Judges of the Supreme Court, and all other Officers of the United States, whose Appointments are not herein otherwise provided for, and which shall be established by Law: but the Congress may by Law vest the Appointment of such inferior Officers, as they think proper, in the President alone, in the Courts of Law, or in the Heads of Departments.

Clause 3: The President shall have Power to fill up all Vacancies that may happen during the Recess of the Senate, by granting Commissions which shall expire at the End of their next Session.

Section. 3.

He shall from time to time give to the Congress Information of the State of the Union, and recommend to their Consideration such Measures as he shall judge necessary and expedient; he may, on extraordinary Occasions, convene both Houses, or either of them,

Appendix B - The U.S. Constitution

and in Case of Disagreement between them, with Respect to the Time of Adjournment, he may adjourn them to such Time as he shall think proper; he shall receive Ambassadors and other public Ministers; he shall take Care that the Laws be faithfully executed, and shall Commission all the Officers of the United States.

Section. 4.

The President, Vice President and all civil Officers of the United States, shall be removed from Office on Impeachment for, and Conviction of, Treason, Bribery, or other high Crimes and Misdemeanors.

Article. III.

Section. 1.

The judicial Power of the United States shall be vested in one Supreme Court and in such inferior Courts as the Congress may from time to time ordain and establish. The Judges, both of the Supreme and inferior Courts, shall hold their Offices during good Behaviour, and shall, at stated Times, receive for their Services, a Compensation, which shall not be diminished during their Continuance in Office.

Section. 2.

Clause 1: The judicial Power shall extend to all Cases, in Law and Equity, arising under this Constitution, the Laws of the United States, and Treaties made, or which shall be made, under their Authority;--to all Cases affecting Ambassadors, other public Ministers and Consuls;--to all Cases of admiralty and maritime Jurisdiction;--to Controversies to which the United States shall be a Party;--to Controversies between two or more States;--between a State and Citizens of another State; --between Citizens of different States, --between Citizens of the same State claiming Lands under Grants of different States, and between a State, or the Citizens thereof, and foreign States, Citizens or Subjects.

Clause 2: In all Cases affecting Ambassadors, other public Ministers and Consuls, and those in which a State shall be Party, the

Supreme Court shall have original Jurisdiction. In all the other Cases before mentioned, the Supreme Court shall have appellate Jurisdiction, both as to Law and Fact, with such Exceptions, and under such Regulations as the Congress shall make.

Clause 3: The Trial of all Crimes, except in Cases of Impeachment, shall be by Jury; and such Trial shall be held in the State where the said Crimes shall have been committed; but when not committed within any State, the Trial shall be at such Place or Places as the Congress may by Law have directed.

Section. 3.

Clause 1: Treason against the United States shall consist only in levying War against them, or in adhering to their Enemies, giving them Aid and Comfort. No Person shall be convicted of Treason unless on the Testimony of two Witnesses[82] to the same overt Act, or on Confession in open Court.

Clause 2: The Congress shall have Power to declare the Punishment of Treason, but no Attainder of Treason shall work Corruption of Blood, or Forfeiture except during the Life of the Person attainted.

Article. IV.

Section. 1.

Full Faith and Credit shall be given in each State to the public Acts, Records, and judicial Proceedings of every other State. And the Congress may by general Laws prescribe the Manner in which such Acts, Records and Proceedings shall be proved, and the Effect thereof.

Section. 2.

---

82 *Deuteronomy 17:6; 2 Corinthians 13:1*

Clause 1: The Citizens of each State shall be entitled to all Privileges and Immunities of Citizens in the several States.

Clause 2: A Person charged in any State with Treason, Felony, or other Crime, who shall flee from Justice, and be found in another State, shall on Demand of the executive Authority of the State from which he fled, be delivered up, to be removed to the State having Jurisdiction of the Crime.

Clause 3: No Person held to Service or Labour in one State, under the Laws thereof, escaping into another, shall, in Consequence of any Law or Regulation therein, be discharged from such Service or Labour, but shall be delivered up on Claim of the Party to whom such Service or Labour may be due.

Section. 3.

Clause 1: New States may be admitted by the Congress into this Union; but no new State shall be formed or erected within the Jurisdiction of any other State; nor any State be formed by the Junction of two or more States, or Parts of States, without the Consent of the Legislatures of the States concerned as well as of the Congress.

Clause 2: The Congress shall have Power to dispose of and make all needful Rules and Regulations respecting the Territory or other Property belonging to the United States; and nothing in this Constitution shall be so construed as to Prejudice any Claims of the United States, or of any particular State.

Section. 4.

The United States shall guarantee to every State in this Union a Republican Form of Government, and shall protect each of them against Invasion; and on Application of the Legislature, or of the Executive (when the Legislature cannot be convened) against domestic Violence.

Article. V.

The Congress, whenever two thirds of both Houses shall deem it necessary, shall propose Amendments to this Constitution, or, on the Application of the Legislatures of two thirds of the several States, shall call a Convention for proposing Amendments, which, in either Case, shall be valid to all Intents and Purposes, as Part of this Constitution, when ratified by the Legislatures of three fourths of the several States, or by Conventions in three fourths thereof, as the one or the other Mode of Ratification may be proposed by the Congress; Provided that no Amendment which may be made prior to the year One thousand eight hundred and eight shall in any Manner affect the first and fourth Clauses in the Ninth Section of the first Article; and that no State, without its Consent, shall be deprived of its equal Suffrage in the Senate.

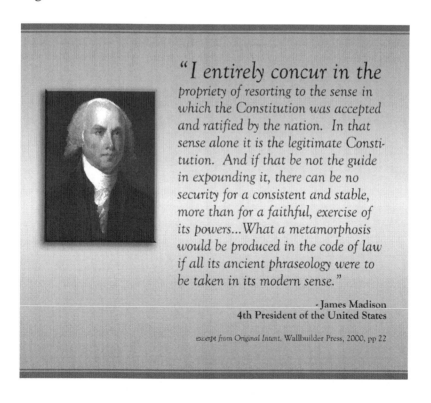

"I entirely concur in the propriety of resorting to the sense in which the Constitution was accepted and ratified by the nation. In that sense alone it is the legitimate Constitution. And if that be not the guide in expounding it, there can be no security for a consistent and stable, more than for a faithful, exercise of its powers...What a metamorphosis would be produced in the code of law if all its ancient phraseology were to be taken in its modern sense."

- James Madison
4th President of the United States

excerpt from Original Intent, Wallbuilder Press, 2000, pp 22

Appendix B - The U.S. Constitution

Article. VI.

Clause 1: All Debts contracted and Engagements entered into, before the Adoption of this Constitution, shall be as valid against the United States under this Constitution, as under the Confederation.

Clause 2: This Constitution, and the Laws of the United States which shall be made in Pursuance thereof; and all Treaties made, or which shall be made, under the Authority of the United States, shall be the supreme Law of the Land; and the Judges in every State shall be bound thereby, any Thing in the Constitution or Laws of any State to the Contrary notwithstanding.

Clause 3: The Senators and Representatives before mentioned, and the Members of the several State Legislatures, and all executive and judicial Officers, both of the United States and of the several States, shall be bound by Oath or Affirmation, to support this Constitution; but no religious Test[83] shall ever be required as a Qualification to any Office or public Trust under the United States.

Article. VII.

The Ratification of the Conventions of nine States shall be sufficient for the Establishment of this Constitution between the States so ratifying the Same. Done in Convention by the Unanimous Consent of the States present the Seventeenth Day of September in the year of our Lord one thousand seven hundred and Eighty seven[84] and of the Independence of the United States of America the Twelfth.

---

83   This clause, as well as the First Amendment , shows that the Founders were seeing to it that there would be no establishment of a State religion, but instead, the freedom for everyone to peaceably assemble to freely exercise and practice their religion.

84   Many official American documents of that time stated "in the year, XXXX." Others used the phrase, "In the year of the Lord, XXXX." But in the Constitution, the Founding Fathers deliberately declared "in the year of *our* Lord, XXXX," thus personalizing their identification with Christ. In fact, Founding Fathers who afterward became U.S. presidents even signed government documents using the phrase "in the year of our Lord Jesus Christ." - excerpt from *The Founders Bible.* p 1545.

Prayer For The Nation   -   Mary Ervasti

Your Notes:

Appendix B - The U.S. Constitution

Amendments to the Constitution

ARTICLES IN ADDITION TO, AND AMENDMENTS OF, THE
Amendments to the Constitution
CONSTITUTION OF THE UNITED STATES OF AMERICA, PROPOSED BY CONGRESS, AND RATIFIED BY THE LEGISLATURES OF THE SEVERAL STATES, PURSUANT TO THE FIFTH ARTICLE OF THE ORIGINAL CONSTITUTION

Article [I.]

Congress shall make no law respecting an establishment of religion, or prohibiting the free exercise thereof; or abridging the freedom of speech, or of the press; or the right of the people peaceably to assemble, and to petition the Government for a redress of grievances[81].

Article [II.]

A well regulated Militia, being necessary to the security of a free State, the right of the people to keep and bear Arms, shall not be infringed.

Article [III.]

No Soldier shall, in time of peace be quartered in any house, without the consent of the Owner, nor in time of war, but in a manner to be prescribed by law.

---

81 On every question of construction, carry ourselves back to the time when the Constitution was adopted, recollect the spirit manifested in the debates, and instead of trying what meaning may be squeezed out of the text, or invented against it, conform to the probable one in which it was passed.
   Admonition to Supreme Court Justice William Johnson by Thomas Jefferson, Third President of the United States
   excerpt from Original Intent, Wallbuilders, 2000, *p. 22*
   Galatians 6:7-8

As a matter of public record, the delegates [to the Constitutional Convention] included 28 Episcopalians, 8 Presbyterians, 7 Congregationalists, 2 Lutherans, 2 Dutch Reformed, 2 Methodists, 2 Roman Catholics, 1 unknown, and 3 deists. A full 93% of its members were members of Christian churches, and all were deeply influenced by a Biblical view of mankind and government.
   excerpt from The American Patriot's Bible, *p. 1-11*

Article [IV.]

The right of the people to be secure in their persons, houses, papers, and effects, against unreasonable searches and seizures, shall not be violated, and no Warrants shall issue, but upon probable cause, supported by Oath or affirmation, and particularly describing the place to be searched, and the persons or things to be seized.

Article [V.]

No person shall be held to answer for a capital, or otherwise infamous crime, unless on a presentment or indictment of a Grand Jury, except in cases arising in the land or naval forces, or in the Militia, when in actual service in time of War or public danger; nor shall any person be subject for the same offence to be twice put in jeopardy of life or limb; nor shall be compelled in any criminal case to be a witness against himself, nor be deprived of life, liberty, or property, without due process of law; nor shall private property be taken for public use, without just compensation.

Article [VI.]

In all criminal prosecutions, the accused shall enjoy the right to a speedy and public trial, by an impartial jury of the State and district wherein the crime shall have been committed, which district shall have been previously ascertained by law, and to be informed of the nature and cause of the accusation; to be confronted with the witnesses against him; to have compulsory process for obtaining witnesses in his favor, and to have the Assistance of Counsel for his defence.

Article [VII.]

In Suits at common law, where the value in controversy shall exceed twenty dollars, the right of trial by jury shall be preserved, and no fact tried by a jury, shall be otherwise re-examined in any Court of the United States, than according to the rules of the common law.

Article [VIII.]

Excessive bail shall not be required, nor excessive fines imposed, nor cruel and unusual punishments inflicted.

Appendix B - The U.S. Constitution

Article [IX.]

The enumeration in the Constitution, of certain rights, shall not be construed to deny or disparage others retained by the people.

Article [X.]

The powers not delegated to the United States by the Constitution, nor prohibited by it to the States, are reserved to the States respectively, or to the people.[82]

[Article XI.]

The Judicial power of the United States shall not be construed to extend to any suit in law or equity, commenced or prosecuted against one of the United States by Citizens of another State, or by Citizens or Subjects of any Foreign State.

Article [XII.]

The Electors shall meet in their respective states, and vote by ballot for President and Vice-President, one of whom, at least, shall not be an inhabitant of the same state with themselves; they shall name in their ballots the person voted for as President, and in distinct ballots the person voted for as Vice-President, and they shall make distinct lists of all persons voted for as President, and of all persons voted for as Vice-President, and of the number of votes for each, which lists they shall sign and certify, and transmit sealed to the seat of the government of the United States, directed to the President of the Senate;--The President of the Senate shall, in the presence of the Senate and House of Representatives, open all the certificates and the votes shall then be counted;--The person having the greatest number of votes for President, shall be the President, if such number be a majority of the whole number of Electors appointed; and if no person have such majority, then from the persons having the highest numbers not exceeding three on the list of those voted for as President,

---

82 I consider the government of the United States [the federal government] as interdicted by the Constitution from intermeddling results not only from the provision that no law shall be made respecting the establishment or free exercise of religion [the First Amendment], but from that also which reserves to the States the powers not delegated to the United States [the Tenth Amendment]. Certainly no power to prescribe any religious exercise or to assume authority in any religious discipline has been delegated to the General [federal] Government. It must then rest with the States.
Thomas Jefferson, *Third President of the United States*

the House of Representatives shall choose immediately, by ballot, the President. But in choosing the President, the votes shall be taken by states, the representation from each state having one vote; a quorum for this purpose shall consist of a member or members from two-thirds of the states and a majority of all the states shall be necessary to a choice. And if the House of Representatives shall not choose a President whenever the right of choice shall devolve upon them, before the fourth day of March next following, then the Vice-President shall act as President, as in the case of the death or other constitutional disability of the President. The person having the greatest number of votes as Vice-President, shall be the Vice-President, if such number be a majority of the whole number of Electors appointed, and if no person have a majority, then from the two highest numbers on the list, the Senate shall choose the Vice-President; a quorum for the purpose shall consist of two-thirds of the whole number of Senators, and a majority of the whole number shall be necessary to a choice. But no person constitutionally ineligible to the office of President shall be eligible to that of Vice-President of the United States.

Article [XIII.]

Section 1. Neither slavery nor involuntary servitude, except as a punishment for crime whereof the party shall have been duly convicted, shall exist within the United States, or any place subject to their jurisdiction.[83]

Section 2. Congress shall have power to enforce this article by appropriate legislation.

Article [XIV.]

Section 1. All persons born or naturalized in the United States, and subject to the jurisdiction thereof, are citizens of the United States and of the State wherein they reside. No State shall make or enforce any law which shall abridge the privileges or immunities of citizens of the United States; nor shall any State deprive any person of life, liberty, or property, without due process of law; nor deny to any person within its jurisdiction the equal protection of the laws.

Section 2. Representatives shall be apportioned among the sever-

---

83 He who made all men hath made the truths necessary to human happiness obvious to all... Our forefathers opened the Bible to all.
Samuel Adams, *Signer of the Declaration of Independence*

Appendix B - The U.S. Constitution

al States according to their respective numbers, counting the whole number of persons in each State, excluding Indians not taxed. But when the right to vote at any election for the choice of electors for President and Vice President of the United States, Representatives in Congress, the Executive and Judicial officers of a State, or the members of the Legislature thereof, is denied to any of the male inhabitants of such State, being twenty-one years of age, and citizens of the United States, or in any way abridged, except for participation in rebellion, or other crime, the basis of representation therein shall be reduced in the proportion which the number of such male citizens shall bear to the whole number of male citizens twenty-one years of age in such State.

Section 3. No person shall be a Senator or Representative in Congress, or elector of President and Vice President, or hold any office, civil or military, under the United States, or under any State, who, having previously taken an oath, as a member of Congress, or as an officer of the United States, or as a member of any State legislature, or as an executive or judicial officer of any State, to support the Constitution of the United States, shall have engaged in insurrection or rebellion against the same, or given aid or comfort to the enemies thereof. But Congress may by a vote of two-thirds of each House, remove such disability.

Section 4. The validity of the public debt of the United States, authorized by law, including debts incurred for payment of pensions and bounties for services in suppressing insurrection or rebellion, shall not be questioned. But neither the United States nor any State shall assume or pay any debt or obligation incurred in aid of insurrection or rebellion against the United States, or any claim for the loss or emancipation of any slave; but all such debts, obligations and claims shall be held illegal and void.

Section 5. The Congress shall have power to enforce, by appropriate legislation, the provisions of this article.

Article [XV.]

Section 1. The right of citizens of the United States to vote shall not be denied or abridged by the United States or by any State on account of race, color, or previous condition of servitude.

Section 2. The Congress shall have power to enforce this article by appropriate legislation.

Article [XVI.]

The Congress shall have power to lay and collect taxes on incomes, from whatever source derived, without apportionment among the several States, and without regard to any census or enumeration.

Article [XVII.]

The Senate of the United States shall be composed of two Senators from each State, elected by the people thereof, for six years; and each Senator shall have one vote. The electors in each State shall have the qualifications requisite for electors of the most numerous branch of the State legislatures.

When vacancies happen in the representation of any State in the Senate, the executive authority of such State shall issue writs of election to fill such vacancies: Provided, that the legislature of any State may empower the executive thereof to make temporary appointments until the people fill the vacancies by election as the legislature may direct.

This amendment shall not be so construed as to affect the election or term of any Senator chosen before it becomes valid as part of the Constitution.

Article [XVIII].

Section 1. After one year from the ratification of this article the manufacture, sale, or transportation of intoxicating liquors within, the importation thereof into, or the exportation thereof from the United States and all territory subject to the jurisdiction thereof for beverage purposes is hereby prohibited.

Section. 2. The Congress and the several States shall have concurrent power to enforce this article by appropriate legislation.

Section. 3. This article shall be inoperative unless it shall have been ratified as an amendment to the Constitution by the legislatures of the several States, as provided in the Constitution, within seven years from the date of the submission hereof to the States by the Congress.

Article [XIX].

The right of citizens of the United States to vote shall not be denied or abridged by the United States or by any State on account of sex.

Congress shall have power to enforce this article by appropriate legislation.

Article [XX.]

Section 1. The terms of the President and Vice President shall end at noon on the 20th day of January, and the terms of Senators and Representatives at noon on the 3d day of January, of the years in which such terms would have ended if this article had not been ratified; and the terms of their successors shall then begin.

Section. 2. The Congress shall assemble at least once in every year, and such meeting shall begin at noon on the 3d day of January, unless they shall by law appoint a different day.

Section. 3. If, at the time fixed for the beginning of the term of the President, the President elect shall have died, the Vice President elect shall become President. If a President shall not have been chosen before the time fixed for the beginning of his term, or if the President elect shall have failed to qualify, then the Vice President elect shall act as President until a President shall have qualified; and the Congress may by law provide for the case wherein neither a President elect nor a Vice President elect shall have qualified, declaring who shall then act as President, or the manner in which one who is to act shall be selected, and such person shall act accordingly until a President or Vice President shall have qualified.

Section. 4. The Congress may by law provide for the case of the death of any of the persons from whom the House of Representatives may choose a President whenever the right of choice shall have devolved upon them, and for the case of the death of any of the persons from whom the Senate may choose a Vice President whenever the right of choice shall have devolved upon them.

Section. 5. Sections 1 and 2 shall take effect on the 15th day of October following the ratification of this article.

Section. 6. This article shall be inoperative unless it shall have been ratified as an amendment to the Constitution by the legislatures of three-fourths of the several States within seven years from the date of its submission.

Article [XXI.]

Section 1. The eighteenth article of amendment to the Constitution of the United States is hereby repealed.

Section 2. The transportation or importation into any State, Territory, or possession of the United States for delivery or use therein of intoxicating liquors, in violation of the laws thereof, is hereby prohibited.

Section 3. This article shall be inoperative unless it shall have been ratified as an amendment to the Constitution by conventions in the several States, as provided in the Constitution, within seven years from the date of the submission hereof to the States by the Congress.

Amendment [XXII.]

Section 1. No person shall be elected to the office of the President more than twice, and no person who has held the office of President, or acted as President, for more than two years of a term to which some other person was elected President shall be elected to the office of the President more than once. But this article shall not apply to any person holding the office of President when this article was proposed by the Congress, and shall not prevent any person who may be holding the office of President, or acting as President, during the term within which this article becomes operative from holding the office of President or acting as President during the remainder of such term.

Section 2. This article shall be inoperative unless it shall have been ratified as an amendment to the Constitution by the legislatures of three-fourths of the several states within seven years from the date of its submission to the states by the Congress.

Amendment [XXIII.]

Section 1. The District constituting the seat of government of the United States shall appoint in such manner as the Congress may direct:

A number of electors of President and Vice President equal to the whole number of Senators and Representatives in Congress to which the District would be entitled if it were a state, but in no event more than the least populous state; they shall be in addition to those appointed by the states, but they shall be considered, for the purposes of the election of President and Vice President, to be electors appointed by a state; and they shall meet in the District and perform such duties as provided by the twelfth article of amendment.

Section 2. The Congress shall have power to enforce this article by appropriate legislation.

Amendment [XXIV.]

Section 1. The right of citizens of the United States to vote in any primary or other election for President or Vice President, for electors for President or Vice President, or for Senator or Representative in Congress, shall not be denied or abridged by the United States or any state by reason of failure to pay any poll tax or other tax.

Section 2. The Congress shall have power to enforce this article by appropriate legislation.

Amendment [XXV.]

Section 1. In case of the removal of the President from office or of his death or resignation, the Vice President shall become President.

Section 2. Whenever there is a vacancy in the office of the Vice President, the President shall nominate a Vice President who shall take office upon confirmation by a majority vote of both Houses of Congress.

Section 3. Whenever the President transmits to the President pro tempore of the Senate and the Speaker of the House of Representatives his written declaration that he is unable to discharge the powers and duties of his office, and until he transmits to them a written declaration to the contrary, such powers and duties shall be discharged by the Vice President as Acting President.

Section 4. Whenever the Vice President and a majority of either the principal officers of the executive departments or of such other body as Congress may by law provide, transmit to the President pro tempore of the Senate and the Speaker of the House of Representatives their written declaration that the President is unable to discharge the powers and duties of his office, the Vice President shall immediately assume the powers and duties of the office as Acting President.

Thereafter, when the President transmits to the President pro tempore of the Senate and the Speaker of the House of Representatives his written declaration that no inability exists, he shall resume the powers and duties of his office unless the Vice President and a majority of either the principal officers of the executive department or of such other body as Congress may by law provide, transmit within four days to the President pro tempore of the Senate and the Speaker of the House of Representatives their written declaration that the President is unable to discharge the powers and duties of his office. Thereupon Congress shall decide the issue, assembling within forty-eight hours for that purpose if not in session. If the Congress, within twenty-one days after receipt of the latter written declaration, or, if Congress is not in session, within twenty-one days after Congress is required to assemble, determines by two-thirds vote of both Houses that the President is unable to discharge the powers and duties of his office, the Vice President shall continue to discharge the same as Acting President; otherwise, the President shall resume the powers and duties of his office.

Amendment XXVI

Section 1. The right of citizens of the United States, who are 18 years of age or older, to vote, shall not be denied or abridged by the United States or any state on account of age.

Section 2. The Congress shall have the power to enforce this article by appropriate legislation.

Amendment XXVII

No law varying the compensation for the services of the Senators and Representatives shall take effect until an election of Representatives shall have intervened.

Appendix C
The Constitution (additional notes)

During the Constitutional Convention, the debate over representation became hopelessly deadlocked and growing increasingly bitter. God once again had mercy on the affairs of America. This time He used perhaps the least likely (and therefore most arresting) vehicle—the eighty-one year-old philosopher who had, some forty years before, good-humoredly rejected the efforts of his friend George Whitefield to convert him.

At this crucial moment, when there was not a man present who had any real hope of finding an effective solution, it was Ben Franklin who rose to speak. This elder statesman, who was also one of the most prominent physicists of his age, quietly said:

> *In the beginning of the contest with Britain, when we were sensible of danger, we had daily prayers in this room for Divine protection. Our prayers, Sir, were heard, and they were graciously answered. All of us who were engaged in the struggle must have observed frequent instances of a superintending Providence in our favor....And have we now forgotten that powerful Friend? Or do we imagine we no longer need His assistance?*
>
> *I have lived, Sir, a long time, and the longer I live, the more convincing proofs I see of this truth, "That God governs in the affairs of man." And if a sparrow cannot fall to the ground without His notice, is it probable that an empire can rise without His aid?*
>
> *We have been assured, Sir, in the Sacred Writings that except the Lord build the house, they labor in vain that build it. I firmly believe this. I also believe that without His concurring aid, we shall succeed in this political building no better than the builders of Babel; we shall be divided by our little, partial local interests; our projects will be confounded; and we ourselves shall become a reproach and a byword*

Prayer For The Nation - Mary Ervasti

down to future ages. And what is worse, mankind may hereafter, from this unfortunate instance, despair of establishing government by human wisdom and leave it to chance, war, or conquest.

I therefore beg leave to move that, henceforth, prayers imploring the assistance of heaven and its blessings on our deliberation be held in this assembly every morning before we proceed to business.

from **The Light and the Glory** p. 342-343

Your Notes:

Recommended Reading/Listening/Viewing List

Listed items are <u>books</u> except where noted.

For Children

Baby Praise,
*Heirborne**

Baby Praise CD,
*Heirborne**

Baby Praise DVD,
*Heirborne**

God's Awesome Universe DVD,
*Jeff Zweerink/Reasons To Believe**

The Light and the Glory for Young Readers,
*Peter Marshall and David Manuel**

From Sea to Shining Sea for Young Readers,
*Peter Marshall and David Manuel**

Sounding forth the Trumpet for Young Readers,
*Peter Marshall and David Manuel**

Three Cups, A Lesson in Life and Money for Children,
*Tony Townsley and Mark St. Germain**

For Adults

America's Providential History,
Mark A. Beliles and Stephen K. McDowell

American Patriot's Bible,
Thomas Nelson, Inc.*

Faith & Confession: How to Activate Them in Your Life,
Charles Capps*

50 Days of Prosperity Vol. 1,
Gloria Copeland and George Pearsons*

50 Days of Prosperity Vol. 2,
Gloria Copeland and George Pearsons*

5000 Year Leap,
W. Cleon Skousen*

Healing and Wellness Package,
Gloria Copeland*

Journey Toward Creation, DVD
Hugh Ross*

The Light and the Glory,
Peter Marshall and David Manuel*

Recommended Reading

From Sea to Shining Sea,
Peter Marshall and David Manuel*

Sounding forth the Trumpet,
Peter Marshall and David Manuel*

Promise of More than Enough, CD
Kenneth Copeland and Keith Moore*

*Original Intent, The Courts,
The Constitution and Religion,*
David Barton

Prosperity Power Tools,
Dick and Mary Ervasti*

Quantum Faith,
Annette Capps*

Revival Fire,
Wesley Duewel*

Sovereign Framework,
Dick Ervasti*

The Founders' Bible,
Shiloh Road Publishers*

Prayer For The Nation - Mary Ervasti

The Glory of America,
Peter Marshall and David Manuel

The Tongue A Creative Force,
Charles Capps*

* Available for purchase at
www.PrayerForTheNation.com

WEBSITES

Prayer For The Nation, www.PrayerForTheNation.com

Documents of Freedom, WallBuilders, www.WallBuilders.com

The Constitution of the United States, National Center for Constitutional Studies, www.nccs.net

Lexicon of Terms

Body of Christ – all who believe in Christ as Savior and Lord.
1 Corinthians 12:12-27

Declare – to make a strong statement believing it in faith, establishing a decree.
Job 22:28

Respecter of Persons – God does not respect one person more than another. All of us have been given the same measure of faith.
Acts 10:34; Romans 12:3

Righteousness – Doing what's right, because it's right, and doing it right. No excuses, not doing it half way, but all the way right.
Genesis 15:5-7; Deuteronomy 6:25; Philippians 3:9; 2 Timothy 3:16

Salvation Prayer

Father God, I come to you now and ask that You forgive all my sins. I receive that forgiveness and now take the redemption that Jesus paid for on the cross so that I may live with You in heaven forever. I ask for Your Holy Spirit to come in and live in me so that You may direct me from the inside. I receive all the benefits of this salvation from sin and redemption to righteousness through Jesus Christ my Savior. Help me to live in right standing with You from this day forward. I pray this in the name of Jesus Christ, amen.

What to do next?

A message from the author, Mary Ervasti, co-founder of PFTN

If you just prayed this salvation prayer, my husband Dick and I would like to welcome you to the family of God. To help you get started on your Christian experience, we'd like to give you a free gift. It's a bible study in e-book format, *Salvation Is Just The Beginning*. It's an excellent first-look study of the scriptures that gives you a comprehensive understanding of *who you are* in Christ Jesus.

To request your free copy, visit our website at:

www.PrayerForTheNation.com/salvation

Thank you so much for joining us in faith-filled prayer for our nation. We bless you, we bless our nation, and we bless God!

Mary Ervasti is also the author, with her husband Dick Ervasti, of the book

Prosperity Power Tools

Available at:

www.PrayerForTheNation.com/ppt

Made in the USA
Charleston, SC
27 January 2014